This Is Your Season

By Dolores Dotson

Each season is a place of change, and each window is an opportunity for a new beginning. "Windows" is more than a daily walk; it is a lifetime with God. The "windows" of our lives are the time slots we spend each moment of our day

This Is Your Season Ministry
PO Box 206 Rockwall, Texas 75087
www.thisisyourseason.com

Unless otherwise indicated, all scripture quotations are
taken from the New King James Version of the Bible

Library of Congress Cataloging-in-Publication Data
ISBN 13: 978-1530817054
Printed in the United States of America

This Is Your Season

Contents

Table of Contents

Acknowledgments

I could never express my gratitude to those who made this book possible. My first fruit of thanks belongs to God for the indwelling river of wisdom that flows from chapter to chapter. Thank you, God, for Your strength to see this book to the end. To my husband and best friend, Duncan, who labored with from the commencement to the commissioning of this project, your steadfast love and support remained a pillar of strength each time I grew weary. To my children, whom I love so dearly, thank you for your patience and words of encouragement.

To my mother, Audrey Benefield, who has gone home to be with the Lord, and father, William Benefield, who fills me with the knowledge of Christ and blesses me with an inheritance in Him that will never lose its value. I thank God for my family and the church family that was a great support through this process.

To Lisa Evans, a dear friend who worked along-side me to add a touch of love to each chapter. I am also grateful to Lisa for helping me to gather my scattered thoughts and for making this book come to life. It would not exist without her sleepless nights of editing and rewriting. She has embedded her heart into this work.

To Donna Hines, who dared to believe I could do this, thanks for praying to God with me and trusting God for me. To all of my spiritual daughters and sisters in Christ, who have sown their hearts into this book and have been invaluable to me during this time, your love, prayer, and encouragement kept me looking up and pressing forward.

I would like to thank everyone who has played a part in making this book a blessing to others.

Foreword

Each season is a place of change, and each window is an opportunity for a new beginning. "Windows" is more than a daily walk; it is a lifetime with God. The "windows" of our lives are the time slots we spend each moment of our day...

Women often feel down with the cares of life. There was a time in the past when I tried to do everything in my own strength. I was taking care of the needs of the ministry, my family, and working outside of my home. No matter how hard I tried, or how much I gave, for some reason I could never "get it together." On the outside, I appeared to be a role model for other women, but in reality, I was ineffective for everyone during this season of my life. As I began to cry out to God for help, the Lord answered. That is when I discovered that it was my personal season for healing and restoration, as it says in the Psalms: *In the day when I cried out, You answered me, and made me bold with strength in my soul. (Psalm 138:3)*

Each chapter in this book will deal with the different seasons of our lives that God takes us through to draw us closer to Him. Perhaps you will discover that you and I may have gone through similar situations and may have even arrived at the same place, even though the details of our experiences are just like our fingerprints; they distinguish us from everybody else!

Through the years, as I have shared *This Is Your Season* with others, I have discovered that there are two types of women: the unorganized ones, who declare that they cannot follow the principles described in the upcoming chapters to get their lives in order; and the organized ones, who are so regimented with their physical lives that their spiritual lives are in disarray. Regardless of whether you are organized or disorganized, this book can lead you into a real relationship with God, Who never fails. Things that seem imperfect in your eyes, He sees as perfect, because His love for you promises to "...bear all things, believe all things, and hope all things..."

This book does not deal only with your outward struggles; it is meant to help you face the fears within you, so that you can love the real you. Here are some things you will learn to do:

- Maintain a love relationship with God through every season of life.
- Walk with God's presence through each season.
- Abide and rest in God in the midst of your most difficult seasons.
- Develop practical ways to recognize your various seasons.
- Organize your daily life and become more productive for God in all seasons.

This is Your Season will help open your eyes to see that God desires to deal with the root of your problems as He prunes your branches. The root of your problems often stems from past hurts and relationships with your parents, family, friends, or spouse. Since seasons are predestined by God to draw you closer to Him and to conform you into His image, it is imperative for you to pray, study, and meditate on the Scriptures, asking the Holy Spirit for wisdom, so that you can understand what the Lord wants for your life.

In this book, you will learn how to meditate on the Word and allow the Holy Spirit to search the very depths of your heart. Ask God to open up your heart and begin to share with Him your fears, concerns, disappointments, joyful moments, and words of love. I also highly recommend that you start a prayer journal as you read each chapter. There are questions at the end of each chapter that will ask you to view things from your window. Write down whatever you are feeling in your heart as you communicate with Him. Writing in my journal everyday helped me through a lot of my hurts to a place of healing, and I trust that it will be a tool God will use to complete this work in you, too.

CHAPTER ONE
Seasons and Windows

Come to Me, all you who labor and are heavy laden,
and I will give you rest.
Take My yoke upon you and learn from Me,
for I am gentle and lowly in heart,
and you will find rest for your souls.
For My yoke is easy and My burden is light.
(Matthew 11:28)

In addition, He will give the rain for your land
in its season,
the early rain and the latter rain,
that you may gather in your grain,
and your wine, and your oil.
(Deuteronomy 11:14)

The Lord told us that if we will come to Him, He will give us rest. For some reason, it is hard for us to believe His Word is true. Jesus is no longer dead on the cross, but He is living among us right now, with outstretched arms, saying, "Come to Me, Daughter, and I will give you rest for your soul." Our soul consists of our mind, will, and emotions. Jesus wants to carry our load and help us through each moment of our lives.

I can remember being in a place where God wanted to change my season and give me rest for my soul, but I fought with Him. During that season, I had established a women's ministry in a little town in Virginia under the covering of a growing church. This was an awesome time in my life, because He was using me in a mighty way, and I was seeing women's lives change. I was consumed with the responsibility and loved this gentle move of God in this season of my life. Nevertheless, the wind began to blow in another direction during the fall and winter of 1992.

As the winter winds began to blow, my life changed. I was so turned around that I did not know what God was doing, or what season I was entering. God told me to lay down everything that was going on in my life and submit totally to Him. I must admit, I did not submit with joy. I liked the fact that He was using me for His glory, and did not want to leave the ministry work I was doing. Still, the Holy Spirit persisted in telling me to lay down this ministry and follow Him, even though He was the one who gave me the heart for women and the unction to establish the ministry in the first place.

The choice was not easy; I loved Him so much that I wanted to yield to His loving will for my life, so finally I said, "Yes, Lord, do whatever You want with me." Little did I know then, that the Lord was about to take me into a season that was hard, cold, lonely, and painful. I thought I had overcome so many areas in my life already, but the Holy Spirit let me know that He needed to do surgery on me and go into the very depths of my heart.

When we let Jesus into those areas of our lives, we are opening up those hidden parts that we have not allowed anyone to enter, though we often think we have. This was a turning point in my life, and now He wanted to take me through a time of growth in Him. Jesus gently brought me through that season, showing me how much He loves me, and that my worth was in Him, not in man.

Through this process, He was molding and shaping me for something greater. He brought peace and order to my life. As I yielded to Him, the windows of heaven began to pour down blessings I never expected.

Cleaning Windows Can Change Lives

In the summer of August 2000, I spent a weekend with a dedicated group of women from the new ministry in which I was serving. These women worked diligently and faithfully alongside my husband and me, but were always tired and frustrated, and could not seem to "get it together." They all came with an expectation, but no one knew exactly What God was going to do, and neither did I. However, I began by sharing with those women how the Lord had revealed to me a word that would ultimately change the rest of my life: **Windows**. This book got its name in August of 2002.

Windows is more than a daily walk; it is a lifetime with God. The "windows" of our lives are the time slots we spend each moment of our day. For example, if you get up at 5:00 a.m. to pray, and pray until 6:00 a.m., then spend an hour with your children, before they go to school, you have used two time slots, or windows, that morning. I have to get up at 4:00 a.m. to have my window of prayer. If I do not get up at 4:00 a.m., I would lose my window with God, because at 6:00 a.m., my window with my family starts, and I have lost that quiet time of the day, but we will discuss more about windows as you read this book.

We need to understand our seasons and how to survive through each season with the guidance of the Holy Spirit. As long as we are living on this earth, our climatic seasons will always change as God has set them in motion to do, unless God himself changes them. We will always see fall, winter, spring and summer throughout our lives, but that summer, I saw a season of winter in the lives of the most dedicated women I had ever worked with, and they loved the Lord with all their hearts. While working with them, I recognized that they were tired, burned out, and overwhelmed with the ministry and with their personal lives. They needed the wisdom and guidance of the Holy Spirit to help them come into a place of rest in the arms of Jesus.

By giving God the window of time in my life that He deserved, and by applying practical biblical principles, I became more available, more accessible, and more productive for God, and you can, too! God was faithful and began to take me on the journey through each season of my personal life. Our seasons are personal, because He has to deal with some personal issues. I could relate to those women who desired to please God. As I shared with them that weekend, God revealed to me that "windows" is something that women will embrace in their hearts and walk out daily in their lives.

He desires to find the root of our problems, not the branches. The root of our problems comes from the past hurts and relationships that we had throughout our lives. Whether it was our parents, family members, friends, or spouses, somehow they all affect us in one way or another. Before I take you on this wonderful journey through the different seasons of your life, I want to first address what a "window" in your life represents.

A window is an opening in a building, to let in light and air, or through which to look outside. Our bodies are windows through which the Spirit of the Lord shines His light.

> *Or do you not know that your body is the TEMPLE of the Holy Spirit who is in you, whom you have from God and you are not your own? For you were bought at a price. Therefore glorify God in your body and in your spirit, which are*

God's. (1 Corinthians 6:19-20)

You are the LIGHT of the world; a city that is set on a hill cannot be hidden. Let your light so shine before men that they may see your good works and glorify your Father in heaven. (Matthew 5:14-16)

God wants our light to shine before men so that they may see Him, the Living Christ, who dwells in us. When we are bombarded by the cares of the world, however, we find our lives in disarray and completely out of order. The windows of our temples become covered with the soot and grime of weariness and frustration because we do not have enough time to complete the day-to-day routines. If our windows are dirty, then others cannot see into them and glimpse God's light, and we cannot be effective for Him.

One of the major reasons why we are unable to keep the windows of our temple clean is our inability to manage time. In *Psalms 90:12*, we are encouraged to number our days, so that we may gain a heart of wisdom. We only have the present moment in which to live. We should make every effort to ensure that the windows of time in our lives are spent wisely not frivolously. We are granted enough time to get things accomplished, get an education, enjoy family and friends, and perform well in our jobs or ministries. No matter how much time we are given, however, we will not be able to accomplish even the simplest task without the help of the Holy Spirit developing in us a consistent lifestyle of order and structure.

We may spend a great deal of time and effort pursuing God's calling before realizing that we have been chasing after our own ambitions. We must learn to rest in God, believe that God has a perfect plan for our lives, and that He will bring it to pass in His time by His love and grace, not by the sweat of our brow alone. God desires to organize our lives so that we can rest in Him and experience the surpassing peace that only comes from Him.

Many Christians will never fully experience God's blessings because they view resting as wasted time. They have conformed to the philosophy that the harder you work, the more successful you are. This is not a biblical principle, yet many Christians have adopted this mindset, which is quite customary in corporations and businesses.

Jesus knew He only had a short time to do His work in the earth, yet He made it a priority to get alone with God to pray and be refreshed. He worked long hours and pressed through sleepless nights, but He made it a point to emphasize the importance of keeping the Sabbath Day as a day of rest. He was constantly surrounded by crowds of people who were pushing and calling His name, wanting and waiting to be healed and touched by His hands. He always took the time to fellowship with friends and sinners. Jesus recognized His seasons and the need to daily seek God for instructions so that God could get the most out of His window of time.

Most of us do not recognize what season we are in, and therefore have a difficult time transitioning from one season to the next. When we are supposed to be in our spring, our whining and complaining have delayed us in our winter. We let Fall bitterness, filled with hurts and disappointments, rob us of the joys we experienced in the summer. Some of us are fighting with the devil when we should be seeking to have a love relationship with the Lord.

Since we cannot control our spiritual seasons any

more than we can control the natural seasons of time, why not make the decision now to accept our seasons and grow from them? In James 1:2-4 it reads, *"My brethren, count it all joy in your season of various trials, knowing that the testing of your faith produces patience. But let patience have its perfect work, that you may be perfect and complete, lacking nothing."* Every season was designed to make us dependent upon God and complete in Him so that we will lack nothing in our lives.

This Is Your Season can help you to have a passion for God, deliverance from your hurts, and the guidance of the Holy Spirit in your daily life as you learn to enter into God's presence and rest in it with peace. As you continue read, each chapter is designed so that you can find yourself in your season.

Each season is a place of change, and each window is an opportunity for a new beginning. I pray that as you read this book, and as you go on this journey with God, He will reveal to you what season you are in, and how He can open the windows of your life and pour down blessings upon you that will drastically change your life.

I hope you will allow God to organize the windows in your life so that you will be better equipped to handle the demands of work, home, and relationships, while drawing closer, into a more intimate bond with the Lord.

Understanding Your Windows

The alarm clock buzzes at 5:00 a.m. It's Monday morning and you feel like you just laid down. Whoever said weekends were free time to do whatever you wanted must have been living in a Cinderella fairytale. My weekends often looked something like this:

After a grueling eight hours of work on Friday, you still have to work at planning family night. The kids are excited about eating something other than your cooking and afterwards, your husband wants you to stay up late with him to spend quality time with him.

Saturday comes around and so does the laundry, the cleaning, the shopping, surprise birthday parties, and everything else that did not seem to fit in on the other six days of the week. Before you know it, it's Saturday night and you are up late trying to get yourself together for tomorrow. Then you realize that in all your running around, you forgot to pick up your clothes from the dry cleaners, you plan to get up a little earlier in the morning and figure out what to wear to church. You did not plan to find a run in your last pair of stockings, or find out that you cannot fit into the dress you just wore a few months ago. While you are creatively pulling an outfit together you keep telling yourself that yes, Jesus does love you.

A quiet Sunday dinner of baked chicken and rice turns into a smorgasbord when you learn that your husband extended a dinner invitation to another family without consulting you. Your guests finally leave around 8:00 at night, and by 9:00 the kids are in the bed, your husband is drifting off to sleep, and you are up trying to finish your weekend chores before you turn into a pumpkin at the stroke of midnight. Where did the time go? Out the window, that is where!

The windows in our lives are designed to help us put our lives in order so we can do the work God has given us to do, while having the right heart condition toward others. When our lives are out of order, we cannot experience the sovereign peace of God, ruling and reigning in our hearts and homes. Ultimately, God wants to organize our lives, so our light can shine before men that they may see our good works and glorify our Father in heaven.

In this chapter, you will learn that through your

relationship with God, that you can make some practical changes to help you to organize your life so God can use you. As you clean the windows in your life, you will discover how to accomplish some goals. You will:

- know your purpose in the Kingdom of God,
- spend quality time with your family, and
- have peace and stability in your work place.

You Cannot Do It Without The Helper

In the season when God was structuring my windows, the Holy Spirit was faithful to give me the wisdom I needed to organize my life. He is waiting for you to ask Him to help. You must know you cannot do it without the Holy Spirit. This must be imprinted in your soul: YOU CANNOT DO IT! It is not in you to do anything of yourself. When you understand that you cannot do it, half the battle is won. We need the help of the Teacher, the Holy Spirit. *"However when He, the Spirit of truth, has come, He will guide you into all the truth; for He will not speak on His own authority, but whatever He hears He will speak; and He will tell you things to come." (John 16:13)*

The Holy Spirit is here to give us wisdom and guide us in the truth of the Word. When we stop and give our day to the Lord and talk to Him about it, in return the Lord speaks through the Holy Spirit and gives us direction for that day. He is my teacher and friend; I could not do anything without Him. Jesus prayed to the Father that He would send the Holy Spirit to teach us all things and to help us as we walk out our salvation on a daily basis. You must see that you cannot do it on your own. You need the Holy Spirit. Oh, please listen to this scripture and understand what God is telling us.

And we have such trust through Christ

> *toward God. Not that we are sufficient of ourselves to think of anything as being from ourselves, but our sufficiency is from God, who also made us sufficient as ministers of the new covenant, not of the letter but the Spirit; for the letter kills, but the Spirit give life. (II Corinthians 3:4-6)*

First, we must trust God for our lives. Sufficient means adequate, enough, capable for filling a need or requirement. We are not able to accomplish anything within ourselves; we must receive our sufficiency from God. He is our only fulfillment in life. That is why He said that we are...epistles of God who has written on our hearts with the Spirit of the living God, not on tablets of stone but on tablets of flesh, which is of the heart. Our hearts are connected through the love relationship we have with God. The letter of the law is a rule that comes out of our flesh, but now Jesus has come under the new covenant, which is a love relationship. We know we can put our confidence in the Lord because we are ministers and epistles of Him. We must learn what He has commanded us to do in our relationship.

This understanding will come out of a relationship with the Lord, not out of rigid rules about how to bring order to your day. That is why so many people go through time management classes and self help books, but they do not work for them. We cannot order our lives with a rule or to try to meet the demands of others. All people do not work or organize their lives in the same manner. Out of your relationship with the Lord, He will personally help you through His wisdom to work in a way that will fit your personality. He knows your limitations, childhood background, temperament, or whatever you might be dealing with. He is gentle in guiding you through with His love. This is something that will take time; spending time with Him in your secret place.

Organizing My Life So God Can Use Me Effectively

God strongly desires to reveal the biblical principles you need in order to walk out His plan for your life on a day-today basis, but so often, we are too busy for God. Whenever we become that busy, we seriously need to re-examine our priorities. Regardless of how busy we are, when we fail to spend time with God or allow our talents to be used for Him, we rob God. In *Malachi 3:10* it says:

> *"Bring all the tithes into the storehouse (the Church you regularly attend). That there may be food in My House, and try Me now in this, Says the Lord of hosts, If I will not open for you the windows of heaven."*

The tithe refers to more than just money; it also refers to our treasures! God wants us to give our time and talent to the Kingdom of God. We cannot do that if we are unorganized and weary from our uncompleted list of things to do.

In that same scripture, God speaks of opening the window of Heaven to bless His children who are obedient to Him. How willing are we to open the windows of our lives to bless God? Let us face it; we are more likely to open our windows to receive from God, rather than to give to God. Just imagine how much more you could give to God if the windows of your life were organized for His good pleasure.

Seasons and Windows

We must understand the importance of having our windows organized. We have to get off the fast track of life, slow down, and learn the rewards of order and rest for our lives. If not, we will always hear ourselves consistently complaining and praying to the Lord:

- Lord, I cannot do it all!
- I am sorry, Lord, I did not have time to pray or read my Bible today.
- I do not have time for myself.
- I cannot find time to spend with my spouse or my children.
- I was not able to complete all the things I had planned for today.
- I do not have time to go to Church or make it to a church meeting.
- I do not have time to prepare or study for Sunday school.
- I have a hard time working with others.
- I have no patience for disorganization.
- Help me, I am tired and frustrated.

You will always be frustrated with yourself and others around you, because your life is not organized enough to be effective for God and others. I cannot begin to count the number of times I have heard someone say, "I have to give up ministry, or I need to take some time off because..."

- My house is out of order.
- My spouse is upset with me because I spend too much time in the ministry.
- I am going back to school.
- I had to take on a new job.
- My job is too demanding right now.
- I am overwhelmed with all the responsibilities of life.

While these may be very good reasons to discontinue your involvement in ministry, you must recognize that stepping down from ministry does not teach you how to discipline your life! The Lord is the Master teacher, and He wants us to learn how to discipline ourselves; however, most Christians have not been taught how to please God in their day-to-day walk with Him.

Words of Wisdom for Planning Your Windows

- ➢ JUST DO IT!
- ➢ LEARN TO SAY NO.
- ➢ SOMEONE ELSE'S EMERGENCY IS NOT YOUR EMERGENCY, IF IT IS A RESULT OF POOR
- ➢ PLANNING.
- ➢ BE CONSIDERATE OF OTHERS' TIME.
- ➢ SHARE WITH YOUR FAMILY ABOUT THE IMPORTANCE OF REST.
- ➢ TEACH YOUR CHILDREN TO RESPECT YOUR TIME OF REST.
- ➢ LEARN TO LET THE PHONE RING.
- ➢ EVERYBODY HAS TO UNDERSTAND
- ➢ BOUNDARIES.
- ➢ REMEMBER, THIS IS ALL IN LOVE. IF YOU ARE ACTING OUT OF RESENTMENT, HURT, ANGER, OR ANY OTHER FLESHLY ATTITUDE, THEN YOU ARE NOT BEING LED BY THE HOLY SPIRIT. THIS WILL BE A PROCESS.
- ➢ PEOPLE MAKE THE TIME TO DO WHATEVER THEY WANT TO DO.
- ➢ YOUR DAY MAY NOT BE THE SAME AS YOUR SPOUSE'S DAY.

Seasons and Windows

In the back of the book, you will find instructions and a Windows sample to fill out that will help you learn how to structure your day.

My Prayer

Holy Spirit, I know that I cannot do it without You. Please, Lord, I need You to help me schedule out my day, because it is not in me to be able to do this. Teach me how to come to You first in my windows of each day. I know I can only hear from You about your plan to guide me through this day. I pray that I accomplish everything that you have chosen for me to finish in my day with you. Let me be a written epistle to my family and other people I am around in my day. Thank you for helping me to organize my life so that you can effectively use me in your kingdom.

Oh, Lord, how I want to please You and my family in my day-to-day walk. I pray that You will teach me how to rest and abide in You. Help me organize my life so that You can use me in my home, on my job, and in the ministry. Teach me how to walk in love as I learn to give my gifts and talents to others who might need my help. Do not let me have a critical attitude toward others, but one of patience and gentleness.

It is my desire to witness to others by allowing the windows of my life to be clean and open for others to see. Help me to maintain a heart after Your heart, with a willingness to put down my own agenda in order to help others. Lord, I pray that You will shine Your light brightly through the windows of my temple every day. Thank You for this new beginning of peace and order in my life.

What Is the View from Your Window?

1. Write down what season in your life you think you are in right now. What evidences do you see to cause you to think this?

2. Begin journaling, and express to God in your journal how you feel about this season and how you need His help.

3. Can you hear the voice of the Lord Jesus saying to you, "Come to Me and I will give you rest?" Stop for a minute and give Him your life of worries and burdens. Lay them down by casting your care down in prayer. Then write a list of those things you have given to Him, and let Him begin to take you through a journey of rest from these cares, worries, and burdens.

CHAPTER TWO
The Season of Knowing the Love of God

*"To know the love of Christ which passes knowledge;
that you may be filled with all the fullness of God."
(Ephesians 3:19)*

On the track of a local junior high school, a mother was playfully chasing her two-year-old daughter. The little girl, looking back at the mother but running forward, laughed freely as her arms swung aimlessly by her side.

As she drew closer to her father standing nearby on the sidelines, he stooped down to a position of gentleness and widened his arms.

Knowing the affection of her father's tender embrace, she disregarded her mother and exerted her energy into racing towards the father. When she reached him, he swept her up in his arms and raised her high in the air as if to say, "You're Daddy's little girl." He then brought her bubbly face close to his and kissed her rosy cheek.

Likewise, we must learn to focus on what's ahead, instead of what's behind us, so that we, too, can come face to face with our loving heavenly Father, who is stooping down to embrace us: *"You give me your shield of victory; you stoop down to make me great." (2 Sam 22:36 NIV)*

In this season of your life, you must understand that God created us for Himself, and He desires to have a loving relationship with us. There is nothing we can do to earn His love, nor can we fully understand the magnitude of it; nevertheless, we can intimately experience the love of God:

> *"...that you, being rooted and grounded in love, may be able to comprehend with all the saints what is the width*

and length and depth and height to know the love of Christ which passes knowledge; that you may be filled with all the fullness of God." (Ephesians 3:19)

God loves us unconditionally. We can never understand with our natural minds how much He loves us. As we get to know God, His love surpasses our very thoughts and imagination, and He fills us with the fullness of His character. This happens by His grace, not through any of our own works. There is nothing we can do to earn His love or grace. It is pure, divine love from God Himself.

He has created us for Himself so that we can have relationship with Him. Jesus is drawing us in with His love, mercy, and grace. If we rest in His love, we can spend an awesome time of intimacy with Him.

We just read about His passion for us. Now let's look at the Scriptures and learn why He wants to discipline us in this love. Jesus becomes the lover of our soul once we have entered into a covenant relationship with Him, similar to a marriage. Most people don't get to enjoy this part of the relationship because they never seek the intimacy.

When we are preparing for our wedding day, we are so excited and in love with our mate. We enjoy the celebration and festivities leading up to the marriage, but when the excitement dies and is replace with the day to day living, we lose the passion we once had and no longer enjoy each other as we did when we first met. We don't know how to continue this love relationship. We find ourselves asking, "What happened?"

This is when we must learn to love unconditionally. The fruits of longsuffering, love and faithfulness become very important in this season of our lives. The relationship is now one that is not based on physical appearance, feelings, or idealistic perceptions. It is now based on learning to love and accept the other person for who they are, and learning how to renew your passion for each other daily. Now we really get to know each other with all quirks and imperfections.

Are we willing to continue to love that person in spite of his faults and in the hard times that may come our way? Sometimes those faults and hard times are too much to bear. This is when we really learn how to love our mate with the love of God.

The Bible gives us a list of what unconditional love is all about in 1 Corinthians 13. This is our goal and pattern for our lives. *"And though I have the gift of prophecy and understand all mysteries and all knowledge, and though I have all faith, so that I could remove mountains, but have not LOVE I am nothing...(1 Corinthians 13:2-8)*

The Lord knew we would need this passage in the Scriptures, so we could understand His definition of love versus our definition of love. We bring into our relationship the definition of love based on Mom and Dad's relationship. We bring the world's view of love relationships modeled on the television. We might have never seen a good relationship in our lives, yet we come into our own relationship with certain expectations.

Well, you are now on a journey to learn the love of the One who created love and masters this love very well. When you come into a love relationship with Jesus, it is the most wonderful love you will ever experience. No man or woman can love you like Jesus. He loved you before you knew Him, and He loved you while you were still a sinner. This love is not based on anything you did. Jesus was willing to die for you even when you rejected His love, because you did not understand. Our entire relationship is based on His awesome love for us.

Even when we turn from God, He passionately pursues us because of His commitment to love us with an everlasting love; *"I will betroth you to Me forever; Yes, I will betroth you to Me in righteousness and justice. In loving-kindness and mercy, I will betroth you to Me in faithfulness and you shall know the Lord."* (Hosea 2:19)

I Will Betroth You to Me Forever

In the book of Hosea, God asked his servant, Hosea, to marry a harlot named Gomer. God knew that she would not be faithful in the marriage, but He wanted to establish a love covenant relationship that mirrored His covenant love for His people. We do not like to see ourselves as Gomer, who was unfaithful. However, if we are honest with ourselves, we will realize that we are very much like her.

Many have ventured from one unhealthy relationship to another, seeking and longing to be fulfilled, just as Gomer did. When these relationships ended, we were left dragging emotional baggage, filled with shameful memories of our lovers, the lust associated with those empty relationships, and the disappointments that followed. Often we are so driven by our own desire to be loved, we do not even realize that we have exchanged love for lust; holiness for happiness; and God for gods.

Sure, we keep the traditions. We attend church, sing songs, and tell God how much we love Him; however, our heart's motivations and actions reflect a lifestyle that does not please Him. Jesus told the Scribes and Pharisees that they honored their traditions, but not God: *"These people draw near to Me with their mouths and honor Me with their lips, but their heart is far from Me. And in vain they worship Me. Teaching of doctrines the commandments of men."* (Matthew 15:7-9)

Likewise, our hearts are often far from God. We have replaced a relationship with Christ with a greater devotion to our jobs, the ministry, furthering our education, and the pursuit of our own personal dreams and achievements. Wanting to improve yourself is never a bad decision, but it can become an unwise choice when you become the center focus, and God is kindly asked to sit in the backseat of your life. When we come to this point in our relationship with God, we do not spend time reading the Word, fasting, and praying, because we have managed to believe that spending quality time with God infringes on the time we have designated for the more immediate pleasures of life. In reality, any desire that we have that is greater than a desire for God is nothing more than an idol. Unfortunately, before we realize it, these desires not only consume us but control us as well.

Each day we are faced with making decisions, and the choices we make determine the outcome of a particular situation and even the destiny of our lives. Gomer chose to chase after her lovers rather than to pursue a genuine relationship with God. Blinded by her own misery, Gomer could not see that the kind of love that her lovers offered was both temporary and costly, but that God's kind of love is eternal and is freely given to each of us: *"God demonstrated His own love toward us in that while we were yet sinners, Christ died for us." (Romans 5:8)*

Is it hard to believe that Gomer wanted to experience the genuine love that Christ demonstrated? Can you imagine what it must have been like for her? Night after night, she subjected her body to the hands of men who cared more about gratifying their fantasies than satisfying her needs. She offered her tender lips to the cracked mouths of men who whispered lies they thought she wanted to hear, giving her heart to the emotional roller coaster ride that was always speeding down, never up.

Just picture this young woman, touched but never felt, hugged but never held, fondled but never caressed, desired but never cared for. How could men's hollow words: "You're beautiful"... "You're special"...or "Of course, I love you" fill the emptiness she was experiencing?

As she lies beside her lover, with disheveled hair and tears streaming down her face, she contemplates quitting. She is tired, but she is not accustomed to the kind of intimacy her husband wants to lavish on her. Finally, she gathers her things and leaves, hoping the next man will be different.

We, too, can become so bound by the hurts, disappointments, and failures of broken covenants that we have a difficult time believing that we can ever experience God's love. In fact, for some of us, we are so unfamiliar with love that we are no longer convinced that it really even exists. Gomer tried desperately to find love, but she continued to look in all the wrong places. We could consider this a winter season for Gomer, because it was a hard and cold time for her. The emptiness she faced in each broken relationship was no doubt painful, but it also left her unprepared for the winter storm blowing her way. The season of winter proved to be a very hard and cold place for Gomer to find refuge. The season of winter is a painful time in our lives, when we look for love and are disappointed in every new relationship.

One possible reason Gomer experienced failure with love may have been that her parents did not exhibit real love to her, perhaps because they did not know how to love God's way. As children, many of us did not have parents who had a loving covenant relationship with God and knew how to demonstrate unconditional love toward us. Instead, our parents loved us as best they knew how or chose to, based on the kind of love they had received from their parents.

Baggage We Carry from Place to Place

Whatever the reasons that contributed to Gomer's folly, if we were to dig deeper into her past, we would find the root of the problem and discover that she has been carrying it around like baggage. Baggage simply represents those things in your past that hinder you from walking in the fullness of God. We all have baggage, and some have more than others do. In addition, we all have need of God's helping hand in unpacking our baggage. In doing so, we will be able to learn to love unconditionally, walk in humility, forgive others, receive the healing balm of God in the broken areas of our lives, and accept the love of God as a gift, and not something we must try to earn.

What conditions or situations have occurred in our lives, which may have contributed, to our baggage? Maybe some of these apply to you:

1. Lack of understanding and accepting the love of God.
2. A broken home or a single parent home.
3. Emotional, spiritual, or physical abuse, which often results in loneliness and emptiness.
4. Generational curses passed on because of the sins of our family and ancestors.
5. Inability to find your identity in Christ instead of man.
6. Battling bouts of loneliness, lack of fulfillment, and dissatisfaction.
7. Victim of incest, rape, or molestation.
8. Rejection, neglect, or abandonment.
9. Vengeance.
10. Little or no display of love, compassion, or

emotional support from parents.

People often bring their baggage into their relationships, including marriages, and struggle to understand and demonstrate unconditional love. When married couples find that they are no longer captivated by their spouse's physical appearance, they tend to focus on the lack of passion instead of pursuing real love. In a period of crisis in a couple's marriage, they may also find that they do not know how to renew the initial excitement in their marriage. Unfortunately, instead of praying, fasting, and seeking Godly counsel, they contemplate ending their marriage because of irreconcilable differences. All kinds of abuse from the past can cause a marriage to end when problems surface, because we do not understand the root of the actual problem.

Embrace His Love

If an individual has been abused at some season in her life, she may convince herself that it was her fault. Subconsciously, she embraces what her conscious mind is unwilling to admit. For example, a wife who believes that her husband's verbal abuse is an acceptable form of love and communication may blame herself for his behavior, instead of identifying that he has a problem. For years she may have blamed herself for her husband's discontentment with her, conditioned to believe that she deserves the life she lives.

No matter how popular, successful, or financially secure a person may be; EVERYONE HAS FAULTS. No one deserves to be mistreated, neglected, or abused because of his or her faults. No one! In the eyes of the Lord Jesus Christ, we are all precious to Him, no matter what our condition may be. He establishes our value; we do not, and certainly, other people do not.

Nevertheless, when we are not aware of the abuse we have encountered, or pretend that it doesn't exist, we cannot understand the beauty of God's unconditional love for us. Even if we reject Christ's love, we still cannot deny that His death on the cross was the ultimate sacrifice and expression of love. Why can we not just embrace Jesus' love and accept it as truth? Because, we are constantly at war with our thoughts, our failures, and the enemy.

An abused child is often the product of a dysfunctional family. As an adult, he will rarely have the desire to reopen past hurts. But the enemy, on the other hand, delights in stirring up your past as a means to devalue you. His strategy is to keep you defeated, and in order to achieve his goal, he has to fill you with fear, despair, depression, and all kinds of thoughts to prevent you from experiencing victory through the love of God. He wants to keep you from loving yourself and knowing your worth in Christ Jesus.

Recognize Your Enemies

Our Father in heaven wants us to know Him, so He can fill us with His love. As the Lord begins to fill us with His love, He allows us to go through some testing. This is important to understand, because if we don't, the enemy will put in our minds that it is God's fault. We will begin to hear the enemy's voice telling us, "He allowed your child or family member to die... that is why your husband left you...If He loves you so much, why are you struggling in your finances...why are you about to be put on the streets? We begin to believe the thoughts and to become angry with God; therefore, we allow ourselves to be in the position where it is difficult to embrace God's love.

We just need to know what enemy we are battling.

When the devil stands as our accuser, we must turn to the Lord for our weapons of warfare. Often, God gives us the weapon of "trials" to defeat our enemies. The enemy works overtime in our mind, trying to convince us that God is not for us, but against us. He wants to weaken our faith, rob us of our inheritance, and ultimately destroy our relationship with God. In the hand of the enemy, trials are used to strike fear and render us helpless, but in the hand of God, trials are used to strengthen us and bring us victoriously through every storm. God allows us to endure trials for His glory. Through our experience and obedience to the Holy Spirit, not only are we encouraged, but we strengthen others, also.

If we believe the lies of the devil and the pain of our flesh, we put ourselves in a position where it is difficult to embrace God's love. We will become angry with God, ineffective in our prayer time and Bible study. Eventually, our attendance in church will decrease. When our enemy, the devil, and our flesh whisper lies in our ears concerning our heavenly Father and our position in the Kingdom of God, we must remember that his whole purpose is to steal, kill, and destroy. Jesus said, *"I have come that they may have life, and that they may have it more abundantly." (John 10:10)*. God's love has the power to overcome every difficult trial you will encounter in any relationship.

A Love that Never Fails

In I Corinthians 13:4-8, God grants us insight into the real meaning of love:

> *"Love suffers long and is kind; love does*
> *not envy; love does not parade itself, is*
> *not puffed up; does not behave rudely,*

26

does not seek its own, is not provoked, thinks no evil; does not rejoice in iniquity, but rejoices in the truth; bears all things, believes all things, hopes all things, endures all things. Love never fails."

This love only comes through abiding with the Lord in His secret place of love. We must seek Him so we can flow in His river of love. If we can apply these truths concerning love in our relationships, instead of the world's view of love, we can be an example of unconditional love for others.

The Father Loves His Children

We usually model our relationships based on what we have seen in others, such as our parents, relatives, friends or co-workers. Regardless of the success or failure in other relationships, we must understand that God is not interested in cloning these relationships in us. He wants us to experience the unique personal intimacy of genuine love.

There is no greater love than that which our heavenly Father has for us. God strongly desires an intimate relationship with us so that He can fill us with His love. One way that God fills us with His love is by testing our faith through trials and tribulations. He designs the trials we encounter to strengthen our faith, reveal the motivation of our heart, and draw us closer to Him. You may question the love of God if you, or someone you know, has suffered greatly because of trials. You may even ponder, how can God allow this to happen if He loves me?

Let us look at this from an earthly parental

perspective. Children do not always agree with how their parents demonstrate love; the tight-reign of discipline may seem more like punishment than love. The parents are responsible for setting the example, establishing a spiritual foundation, and developing the moral structure of their children, which includes respect, honor, and obedience to the parent, others, and to God. When a parent asks their child, "Where have you been? Who were you with? What were you doing?" it is not because they want to limit or hinder their child's creativity, potential, or abilities. Rather, the parents want to establish a healthy environment in which the child can safely grow into a strong, healthy, successful, mature adult.

God desires to move in our lives in the same manner. God does not use the trials in our lives to destroy us, but to strengthen us and establish us in His Word so that we can prosper by overcoming the things of the world. As we accept this truth, we find that even in the worst circumstances, God will never forsake us.

When we recognize that God's love and His presence are right alongside us through every trial, we gain understanding into *Romans 5:3-5:*

> *"But we also glory in tribulations, knowing that tribulation produces perseverance; and perseverance, character; and character, hope. Now hope does not disappoint, because the love of God has been poured out in our hearts by the Holy Spirit who was given to us."*

It is not easy to rejoice in tribulation if you do not understand how you can grow from it. I learned this firsthand after I had been married for a couple of years.

The trials and tribulations that came my way were so overwhelming; I thought my marriage was under attack by every force in the kingdom of darkness. When the demands of being a wife and mother became too much for me to bear, I desperately cried out to God. It was then that the Holy Spirit drew me into my prayer closet for communion with Him. There, I found the love of God waiting to embrace me and minister to my needs. With tearful eyes, I opened my heart to the Holy Spirit and through the Word of God; He opened His loving arms to me. God's love was revealed to me in the midst of my brokenness. I knew He loved me, but it became more and more evident just how much He loved me every day. He refused to leave me in my broken condition.

He Still Loves Me

The situations I faced in my marriage have taught me how to persevere, love unconditionally, press into the love of God through prayer, and to have hope and faith in God. I can recall a trial in my marriage when God revealed something to me that changed the course of my life and the destiny of my marriage.

I was at a woman's retreat when I experienced a breath-taking encounter with the love of God. It was so powerful, that the more He embraced me with His loving arms, the more I wanted to embrace Him. I could barely wait for an interval in the meeting to share my excitement with my husband. As soon as he heard my voice on the phone, he immediately began to demand the reason or the condition of our checking account, which I was managing at the time. Balancing the checking account was not a difficult task, but my lack of discipline in recording the transactions and keeping an update on the current balance made the job extremely challenging and frustrating. Nonetheless, I did not feel that my actions warranted the insensitive words my husband hurled at me. Though I was apologetic, I was also convinced that once I cleaned up the account, I was gladly handing it over to him to balance from that point forward.

After I hung up the phone, I returned to the retreat and found that God was still allowing me the grace to bask in His Presence. As I sat there trying to settle the matter in my mind, God was busy settling the issues of my heart. He revealed to me how the hidden junk in my life: insecurity, fear, lack of discipline, and deception, were causing the deterioration of my marriage.

God made it perfectly clear that because of my lack of integrity, I had written a blank check for the enemy to come in and attack my marriage through our finances. I could not even blame the devil for what had happened.

I thought my repentance to my husband and to God was appropriate, but when God shined His light on the pious attitude of my heart, I realized that He was not looking for the shallow repentance of a religion. He was looking for the sacrifice of true repentance of the heart. *"The sacrifices of God are a broken spirit, a broken and contrite heart. These, O God, You will not despise." (Psalms 51:17)*

If we do not lock into a love relationship with God, we will not be able to surrender to the One who is calling and drawing us with His loving kindness. We must humble ourselves and submit to the discipline of the Lord in order to experience the change that must take place if we are to be like Christ. In *Hebrews 12:5-7*, it says:

> *"My son, do not despise the chastening of the Lord, Nor be discouraged when you are rebuked by Him; For whom the Lord loves He chastens, And scourges*

every son whom He receives. If you endure chastening, God deals with you as he would one of His sons; for what son is there whom a father does not chasten?"

Remember, God does not use discipline to express His dissatisfaction with us, but to demonstrate His love for us. Therefore, we can surrender ourselves to the chastening of the Lord, knowing that His discipline is leading us on the path to holiness. This was my season to know a loving God who loved me in spite of my flawed character, so much that He wanted to change my character into His image. It is hard to move on to the next season of life and be effective for God if you do not allow Him to deal with your heart and to pour His awesome love into you. Stop for a few moments and pray this prayer with me before moving on to the next season.

My Prayer

Father, even when I fail to draw near unto You, continue to draw me unto Yourself so that I may forever experience the beauty of Your unconditional love. Fill me with all of You, until my cup runs over. I so desire to embrace Your love, but I fear that my past hurts and failures have me trapped. Even now, I can see how the hurtful words of others have caused me to think less of them, but also, less of myself.

Lord, soften the callousness of my wounded heart through the power of forgiveness. In this winter season, teach me how to love myself, to understand that my worth is in You, and that You deeply love me for who I am. Help me to understand how Your love is revealed to me through Your death on the cross. Surely, I am valuable in your sight, because You paid the ultimate price for me to be free. Keep reminding me that I am the apple of Your eye, and that You have the very best in store for me because You decided that is what I deserve.

What Is The View from Your Window?

1. In this season of your life, have you been seeking the love of God or man? Ask the Holy Spirit to search your heart, and be honest with yourself.

2. Do you find yourself like Gomer, looking for love and acceptance, but never seeming to fill that empty void in your life?

3. List some things in your life that you consider baggage that hinders you from understanding the love of God.

4. Are you willing to allow God to heal your hurts in this season by surrendering all of them to Him today? If you said yes, stop for a minute and pray. Surrender all your hurts of the past so you can move on to the next season of your life.

CHAPTER THREE
The Season of Accountability

*"Greater love has no one than this, than
to lay down one's life for his friends. You are
My friends if you do whatever I command you."*
(John 15:1)

For over ten years, I have listened to the cries from women with wounded hearts scarred by marital problems, physical and emotional abuse, and low self-esteem. At the end of each counseling session, I give specific instructions on becoming the victor instead of the victim. I always stress the importance of accountability.

I have dealt with a number of women who seem to view accountability as something they need only in a crisis or when things have gotten out of control. It is an unfortunate situation when it gets to this point, because much of their hardship could have been prevented if only they had made themselves accountable. In *Hosea 4:6*, the word of the Lord is spoken through the prophet Hosea: *"My people are destroyed for lack of knowledge."*

The knowledge that is spoken of in this verse represents spiritual knowledge. We must pray for friendship and healthy accountability relationships. We should be accountable to someone who is mature, godly, and chosen by God. When the woman to whom you can be accountable is revealed to you, she will be a woman of character and integrity, as described in *Titus 2:3-5:*

> *"The older women likewise, that they
> be reverent in behavior, not slanderers,
> not given to much wine, teachers of
> good things- that they admonish the*

> *young women to love their husbands, to love their children, to be discreet, chaste, homemakers, good, obedient to their own husbands, that the word of God may not be blasphemed."*

Look for a woman you can count on to be there for you. She knows how to control her behavior and her emotions. She does not gossip, because she is one who knows how to control her tongue. She does not "party" and allow things of the world to influence her. Her purpose is to teach good things, such as how to love your husband, how to carry yourself as a single woman, and how to raise your children through the hard times. She knows when to be quiet, and she takes care of her home. She has learned how to love and submit to her husband according to this relationship in the Word. She has learned all these things over a period of time in her life. God knew He would need seasoned and trained people who could share their faith about how God brought them through by His Word. When I faced difficult times, I needed someone I could call on to share my failures, just as I would share my successes. I needed someone who would pray for me when I lost my focus and wanted to give up.

Friendship Between Two Women

When I think about accountability and mentoring, I am reminded of the relationship between Ruth and Naomi. These two women overcame some difficult seasons in their lives together, through their commitment to one another, and by the leading of the Holy Spirit.

In the book of Ruth, we find Naomi, Ruth's mother-in-law, in a very difficult season in her life. Tragedy struck her family, and Naomi soon found herself widowed, childless and without any financial support. Faced with the shame of a hopeless future, she encouraged Orpah and Ruth to *"...Go return each to her mother's house. The Lord deal kindly with you as you have dealt with the dead and with me."* Seeing herself as an empty vessel, unable to fill anyone's cup, Naomi continued with great effort to convince her daughters-in-law to return home. When the time came for them to decide their futures, it is not certain what factors weighed the most in their decision making, but we do know that one daughter-in-law returned to her past and the other found her future: Orpah kissed Naomi good-bye, but Ruth clung to her:

> *"Entreat me not to leave you or to turn back from following after you; for wherever you go, I will go; and wherever you lodge, I will lodge; your people shall be my people, and your God, my God. Where you die, I will die, and to there will I be buried. The Lord do so to me, and more also, if anything but death parts thee and me."* (Ruth 1:16-17)

Ruth was determined to receive her blessing and had a desire for a relationship with Naomi. Because of Ruth's relationship with Naomi, she was led to the Lord. When God puts us in a position of influence, we must lead women to the Lord. We must let Him examine our walk and have a desire to give out His love to those who are hurting, wounded, lost, and searching for answers. If we go back and look at *Ruth 1:9*, we will see that Naomi is saying good-bye to her two daughters-in-law. She said to them, *"The Lord grant that you may find rest, each in the house of her husband. So she kissed them, and they lifted up their voices and wept."*

I believe in that moment, Ruth saw that she could not get her rest if she did not move on from her past hurts. In this passage, rest means not only an absence of strife, war, or struggle, but contains the idea of God's blessing bringing personal security to the individual. Going back to their homes, where Orpah and Ruth lived, was not a place of rest but a place of past hurts and emptiness. Ruth chose a journey to go with Naomi to Bethlehem, which means the bread of life. Ruth was going where she would be able to rest and will receive the bread of life to help her grow and excel. We do not know what happened to Orpah, but we can speculate that she did not receive the bread of life, because her gods were false gods. They could not give her rest, eternal life, or comfort to her soul.

This beautiful story also shows the power of accountability, and how God was able to use one woman who called herself Mara, which meant "bitter." Because of Naomi's trials, she was able to help her young daughter-in-law to come into her purpose. Though uncertain about their tomorrow, each day on the road back to Bethlehem granted Naomi the opportunity to mentor and display her strength of character before an eager young Ruth, who learned to glean first from her mother-in-law's field of wisdom. As their confidence in God grew, so did their love for one another, so much so that Naomi made it her priority to seek security for Ruth *(Ruth 3:1)*.

Interestingly, while Naomi's name means "pleasantness," Ruth's name means "friend." A friend is a person one knows well and is fond of; one who is a supporter or sympathizer. Jesus had this to say about friends: *"Greater love has no one than this, than to lay down one's life for his friends. You are My friends if you do whatever I command you." (John 15:12)*

Naomi's love for Ruth was evident, as she willingly laid her life down for her friend. When we do not think only of ourselves and are willing to see the need of others, we can lay our lives down for them. Naomi could have insisted that she could only think of herself, and Ruth would have been just an added responsibility as she began to plan to go back home. Though Naomi's son had selected Ruth as his wife, God chose Naomi to be her mentor. Undoubtedly, Naomi could not see herself as one who could help Ruth, but God, who sees beyond our current situation, knew that if Naomi positioned herself in His will, she would truly eat from the bread of life beyond Bethlehem. As you read the book of Ruth, you can see that God provided for them and took care of them both, because of the step of faith to return to a place of provision.

Naomi put herself in a place where she could hear from God, and instructed Ruth on how to enter into the His presence and be fulfilled by Him. *"So she went down to the threshing floor and did according to all that her mother-in-law instructed her...". (Ruth 3:6)*

Because of Ruth's obedience, both she and Naomi benefited from the power of accountability. Accountability means different things to different individuals. We are not talking about control of one's life, but having the ability to share one's heart with another in honesty. As older women, we can help those who do not have an understanding or direction for their life. For a good healthy accountability relationship, we must maintain an honest relationship, openness of communication, and the ability to be taught.

Wise women must seek God first in order to be filled with the sweet oil of wisdom from the Holy Spirit. As God uses us to lead others, it so important that we lead them to Christ, and not to ourselves. Older women who mentor younger women must be willing to spend personal, quality time with God in order to give wise counsel. Jesus said He made known to us what He heard from the Father. Likewise, we must also come to another place in our relationship with God with an expectation of hearing Him speak to our hearts as we inquire of the Lord.

I can remember being challenged to come to another place in God through my time spent with Him when I was going through the toughest season in my marriage, I had no idea what was happening to me. I guess we can say it was a suffering summer of my life. There were times when it seemed as if I were not going to make it. This was a hard summer for me because I felt like I was suffering in the heat of the battle. I did not have an older woman in my life to help me with my baggage from the past; therefore, I was oblivious to the fact that I had brought my past hurts, pains, and disappointments into my marriage.

Looking back at the healing process that God brought me through, I can see how having an older woman in my life could have helped me understand what season I was going through, what I could expect, and even to reassure me that I would live and not die! Even though we can benefit greatly from wise counsel, not everyone seeks to find someone to whom they may make themselves accountable. Instead, they tend to cultivate relationships with people who will agree with what they believe or who will say what they want to hear. Most of us have either been hurt or betrayed by someone, and we have a hard time trusting others. This will cause us to be drawn to people who will please our flesh and not challenge us to see what we are really struggling with in our lives.

God has raised mature men and women, full of faith, to pray for us, who are anointed to move the heavens through effective prayer. In the book of James 5:13-16, we gain a greater understanding of God's intent for mature Christians in our lives:

> *"Is anyone among you suffering? Let him pray. Is anyone cheerful? Let him sing psalms. Is anyone among you sick? Let him call for the elders of the church, and let them pray over him, anointing him with oil in the name of the Lord. And the prayer of faith will save the sick, and the Lord will raise him up. And if he has committed sins, he will be forgiven. Confess your trespasses to one another, and pray for one another, that you may be healed. The effective, fervent prayer of a righteous man avails much."*

They know how to pray, and they can reach the throne of heaven. He has also anointed them to move heaven through their prayer. He did not say to call your girlfriend or boyfriend, who will either agree with you or criticize you. God wanted us to call on someone who will be effective in their prayers because they live a lifestyle of righteousness before God.

Mature Christians Live a Lifestyle of Righteousness

In order for us to experience the power of accountability, we must rid our mindset of all misconceptions that age is a sure sign of maturity. Just because a person is older in age, that does not necessarily qualify them to be a mentor in our lives. A mature Christian lives a lifestyle of righteousness, which is fruitful before God, and is submitted to Him and His Word. The fruit in our lives is the character of God, which represents both who He is and His holiness. God is love, peace, kindness, longsuffering, goodness, faithfulness, and patience.

This is who He is, and He wants us to be characterized by the same fruit, so that we can inherit the kingdom of God. He tells us, *"And now abide faith, hope, love, these three; but the greatest of these is love."* When we walk in love, people can see who we are in Him. Jesus set a standard in a commandment with the disciples. Jesus told them, *"A new commandment I give to you that you love one another. As I have loved you, that you also love one another. By this all will know that you are My disciples, if you have love for one another."*

We must ask ourselves this question, "Can people see that I belong to Christ and that He has taught me to walk like Him?" This love was a new commandment because it had a new standard. It was not a law or a rule; it was about relationship. We must walk in love so that we can affect other people's lives by our walk with Him. His love should be evident in our lives in these ways:

We should have a servant's love; a selfless love; a sacrificial love; a sweet aroma love; a sold-out love. This love comes to restore everything that the enemy stole from us. When we are not abiding in Christ and being led by the Holy Spirit, we cannot walk in love. When we have not been taught to love, we cannot come to this standard of love.

> *"Therefore be imitators of God as dear children and walk in love, as Christ also as loved us and give Himself for us, an offering and a sacrifice to God for a sweet smelling aroma...". (Ephesians*

5:1-2)

Imitate means to follow the example of, or to reproduce. Jesus wants us to look at Him in His Word and follow Him. He wants to reproduce Himself in us through our abiding in His Word and our prayer. We must die to our own selfish desires and sacrifice our lives to be used by Him. Paul knew that in order for the ministry to be effective, it was necessary for him to be Christ-like and disciplined in his lifestyle: *"...But I discipline my body and bring it into subjection lest, when I have preached to others, I myself should become disqualified...". (1 Corinthians 9:27)*

It is apparent that God wants us to be leaders who will allow the Holy Spirit to develop these fruits in our lives. Otherwise, we will not be effective mentors, teachers, or disciples for the Lord. God is looking for imitators, not imposters. There are, however, many people telling others how they should live according to the Word, when in fact, their lives do not reflect their own counsel. We must ask ourselves these questions: Are we walking in the character of God? Who are we when no one else is looking? Do we discipline ourselves so that we can be qualified by God? Are we allowing Him to develop those fruit in our daily lives? Can He effectively use us in this season of our lives?

James 1:22 instructs us to *"...be doers of the word, and not hearers only, deceiving yourselves."* If we do not follow God's principle concerning this, we cannot expect to be effective in our witness. Whenever we do something other than what we say, we lose the trust of those affected by our double standard lifestyle and we ruin relationships. Again, God is not looking for us to be perfect in order to use us. He simply wants us to apply His word in our lives before we go out and try to minister to others.

Though accountability is a very intricate part of our

spiritual growth, it is rendered powerless when it lacks genuine relationship. Making yourself accountable to someone is more than just telling him or her what is going on in your life. It is establishing a covenant bond that will allow you to be honest, transparent, and vulnerable without the fear that your business will be broadcasted. Undoubtedly, there will be times when you will long for someone to listen and talk, cry and laugh with, as you go through the process of being changed by the hand of God.

God intended for men and women to be in relationship with Him first, and then with one another. We first must understand that we must have a relationship with God first in order to have a healthy relationship with man. God had a good relationship with Adam in the garden and He saw that Adam still needed help here on earth. In Genesis 2:18, after God created Adam, He said, *"It is not good that man should be alone; I will make him a helper comparable to him."* When we fellowship with God and each other, we help each other grow, because we are working together for the same cause; to please and fulfill our purpose in Him. When we learn the value of helping each other accomplish God goals, we will see fulfillment in God's purpose in life.

Learning to Walk Together in The Lord

First John 1:3-4 tells us that when we walk in fellowship (relationship) with God and each other, our joy will be full. *"That which we have seen and heard we declare to you, that you also may fellowship with us, and truly our fellowship is with the Father and with His Son, Jesus Christ. And these things we write to you that your joy may be full."*

God wants our lives to be complete, full of peace and

joy. The dark areas in our lives however, keep us from trusting God and others: insecurities, comfort zones, pride, and stubbornness. Our inability to be transparent with God and others hinders us from breaking free from the sin associated with those dark areas. It is imperative that we ask God to shine His light on these dark areas and heal us from the hurt of the past. Only through His grace and mercy will we be able to push back the tears and press forward into the plan and purpose of God for our lives.

You might be thinking, "but I'm ashamed about the things I've done." It does not matter. God has equipped someone who He has delivered out of the same circumstances that you went through. He will strategically position that person in your life to help you. Remember, we are here for each other. If you have been betrayed before, and you are still having a problem trusting people, you need to pray and ask God to release the healing that will open your heart so you may trust again.

On the other hand, while some people do not go to anyone, others go to everybody with their problems. In no way is this recommended, healthy, or scriptural. Continue to pray about to whom you should be accountable in this season of your life. Allow the Holy Spirit to give you wisdom and lead you in the direction that is best for you. Most of the people you talk to may not care, or might want to use your misfortune simply for gossiping.

We Need Wisdom in Choosing to Whom We Are Accountable

Another important area concerning accountability and relationship that must be addressed, is seeking counsel from the opposite sex. In an innocent time of sharing, we may be unaware that an intimate unhealthy relationship is being established. Whenever we turn to the opposite sex for consistent counseling and sharing the matters of our hearts, we open the door to the enemy to tempt us with lust, fornication, and infidelity. I have seen many single people give in to their lustful desires and engage in sexual relations with their counselors, as well as married couples leaving their spouses to satisfy their sexual desires with their counselor.

Watch it when you, a woman, say, "I can only open up to a man," or as men feel, "women can understand me better." If you see yourself in this example, you need to ask the Lord why you tend to draw to the opposite sex to share your problems. We do not always see the danger of such thoughts, because for some, it is an honest belief in our hearts that it is only a friendship relationship. Many times, those of the same sex have hurt us, and we have had to put up with a lot of drama that results in mess and gossip. We try to guard our hearts and talk to someone who would listen and not bring the drama with them. Usually, a man will listen and understand what we might be going through. That attracts us to them to continue a relationship that could be unhealthy, because we do not know the heart or motivation of that other person. When we come into a love relationship with the Lord, He will reveal your heart to you if you really want to grow and see change in your life. He will also lead you to good and healthy friendship relationships.

My husband and I have made it a rule to always be accountable to one another whenever we talk to people of the opposite sex. He directs the women to me, and I instruct the men to communicate with him. We take the time to do this because we want to protect our marriage against Satan's devices, not because we do not trust one another. We use wisdom in our counseling session, because we have counseled many in these positions that have fallen into the traps and ensnarement of the enemy.

If you are married and in a leadership position, you need to learn how to work as a team with your spouse, or a team of people that will help you to be accountable. This statement is also for single people who are in a leadership position. Please set up a team of people in your congregation or organization that will support each other with men and women that understand accountability. Even though your intentions in counseling may be strictly for ministry, the person you are counseling may have a different agenda.

Determine in your heart to make the necessary changes in your life to receive godly counsel. You cannot do it on your own, and God never intended for you to even try. In Jeremiah 3:15 it says, *"And I will give you shepherds according to My heart, who will feed you with knowledge and understanding."* Oh how wonderful! He has raised up men and women after His own heart, possessing the very knowledge and wisdom we need in order to grow. This is a springtime in our lives, because so much beauty can grow between those we trust and embrace as friends. There is so much growth in being accountable to God first, then to others whom God has chosen to love you through your growing season.

My Prayer

Lord, thank you for teaching me that I need to first be accountable to You and then to a mature person whom you have raised up to help me grow in this season of my life. I know they will not be perfect, but they have a heart for You, and You want them to grow as they help me grow. Deal with the hurt stored in my heart, oh Lord, where I have not learned to trust people with the hidden junk in my life. Search my heart for insecurities, pride, stubbornness, and anything else that will stunt my growth in You. I want to be complete in You.

Lead me to the person to whom You want me to be accountable, and teach me how to be honest, transparent, and teachable. Lord, I need someone who has Your heart and is willing to nurture me with the knowledge of your Word. Lord, as my Shepherd, lead me beside still waters, the very place you have chosen for me to find rest.

What is The View from Your Window?

1. Do you let God know when you are disappointed with others and even with Him at times, when you do not understand this season of your life?

2. Write a letter to God, sharing what you really feel, and how you want to have a better relationship with Him in this season.

3. Do you have someone to whom you are accountable as you grow in this season? Are you growing with this person? If not, stop and ask God, "Why am I still in the same place?"

4. Do you find yourself talking to the opposite sex and feeling more comfortable with them than with those of your own sex?

5. Ask God to search your heart and the motivation of your heart. Did you experience a lack of trust and loyalty in friendships with other girls as you were growing up?

6. Older women, stop and ask yourself the question, "Am I being used effectively by God in my character before other women?"

1. If it is your desire to mentor others, stop and pray to God that your life will be an example to younger women of the faith.

CHAPTER FOUR
The Season of Wisdom from the Holy Spirit

"If any of you lacks wisdom,
let him ask Of God, who gives to all liberally and
without reproach, And it will be given to him."
(James 1:5)

It was two years ago when Anthony shouted at his wife, "I want a divorce." As he slammed the bedroom door shut, the emptiness of their marriage echoed throughout the cold house. The struggles and trials in the past few months seemed to be the *"till death do us part"* of their ten-year covenant relationship. Realizing her marriage was in jeopardy, Katrina delayed every opportunity for career changes and business investments, and focused her attention on her family.

Over the past few months, Katrina had noticed that her husband had changed tremendously. The longing he once had for her was being fulfilled by a new circle of friends that she had never met. She pondered deeply, trying to recall the warning signs indicating that their marriage was in trouble.

The tranquil evenings at home had soon turned into tempestuous nights. The inward rage that he fought against oftentimes demanded that he step outside for a breath of fresh air. On many occasions, he would not return until early mornings just before the break of dawn. To avoid stirring up any arguments or the exchange of harsh words, Katrina tried not to complain. After all, she loved him. What reason did she have to question his love for her? Perhaps it was the discovery of his wedding band tucked away in the top dresser drawer. To the world, this signified his freedom, and to her it was his cowardly way of saying goodbye.

Feeling helpless, she pleaded with him to sit down with her and talk things over. Her tender words of "I'm sorry" and "I love you" only stifled him more. What she had hoped to be a turning point in their marriage ended up being the turning point in her relationship with God. Katrina wanted desperately for her marriage to work, but she did not know what to do. In her quiet time with the Lord, she knelt and asked God for wisdom.

Even though it took two years for their marriage to be restored, Katrina admits that without God's wisdom guiding her, she would have given up. Today, Katrina still remembers the night she cried out to God for help, and the scripture that taught her to have patience in the midst of her storm:

> *"...count it all joy when you fall into various trials, knowing that the testing of your faith produces patience. But let patience have its perfect work, that you may be perfect and complete, lacking nothing. If any of you lack wisdom let him ask of God, who gives to all liberally and without reproach, and it will be given to him." (James 1:2-5)*

Building Spiritual Muscles of Faith

The Lord freely gives wisdom in His word to achieve His character in us. When we are going through the trials of life, we may not understand why it takes so long to get through the testing of our faith, but we can be encouraged to know that we will have the victory, because God is there to help us through every situation. The hard part is waiting. Through our trials, we sometimes have to wait, and in that waiting or perseverance, patience is produced so that we will not lack anything.

People desiring physical muscles may think that they can go to the gym and lift weights for a couple of hours and immediately see rippled results in their abs, or be able to flex their triceps and biceps to improve their image. However, their desire alone cannot produce the results. One thing I like about the love of the Lord is that He wants to help us through every situation. He tells us not to worry, but to be encouraged. We are strengthened by the testing of our faith. He wants us to be strong in what and whom we believe, so He allows us to go through trials to build our spiritual muscles. Now, the hard part is waiting. This waiting produces patience in our lives so we will not lack anything. Just as weights were designed to build our physical muscles, trials were designed to build our spiritual muscles and strengthen us by testing our faith.

In this fast-paced world we live in, businesses and manufacturers have appealed to the consumer through a simple word, "express." Supermarkets have express checkout, eye care promises your lenses within an hour, and food manufacturers have made express meals to be ready in minutes, as you effortlessly cook in the microwave. All of these conveniences were designed to help us function with less patience. As a result, when we find ourselves in a situation like a traffic jam or in a long line at customer service, we cannot handle the waiting because we have become constantly moving. In America's society, patience has been replaced by a short fuse and a hot temper.

We need to understand that patience is designed to develop our spiritual growth. First, the Lord allows us to go through a trial to strengthen our faith in Him. Then, He helps us produce the fruit of patience. Finally, He gives us the wisdom and the tools to help us through the test so we can pass.

Wisdom to Know How to Love

Since God desires for His children to succeed in life, when we ask God for wisdom, we can expect to receive it, as well as the empowerment needed to follow God's instructions. His wisdom consists of principles I will never forget and will always pass on to others.

This reminds me of a season that the Lord had taken me through, a hard course of learning how to love children with His love. I definitely needed His wisdom in this area of my life. In this season, my husband and I had been caring for children by providing foster care for more than twenty years. In that time, we had cared for more than twenty-five children in our home. We had nurtured children from all walks of life, with diverse backgrounds, personalities, and behaviors. Over the years, we had come to know what things to expect and how to make the necessary adjustments to meet the challenges.

One day, my husband and I received a telephone call from an out of state social worker asking us to foster a young teenager. My husband and I had met this teenager before through a relative attending our church, but we had never established a relationship with her. Since children are typically assigned to social workers within the state where they live, the request was very unusual. After much consideration, prayer, and counseling, we decided to pick up the young girl and bring her into our home.

The seven hundred mile road trip was consumed with intercessory prayer for a teenager we barely knew and for our own lives because of the many obstacles we had to conquer. We knew all too well what Paul described in 2 Corinthians 4:8-11:

"We are hard-pressed on every side, yet not crushed; we are perplexed, but not in despair; persecuted, but not forsaken; struck down but not destroyed- always carrying about in the body the dying of the Lord Jesus, that the life of Jesus also may be manifested in our body."

My husband and I received a great deal of personal information concerning the young girl and her past prior to making our decision to take her in. To a certain degree, we thought we were ready for the challenge and the opportunity to make a difference in her life. It was not until some time after she arrived that her past, and a season of suicide attempts, made me realize that I did not know how to care for her. Even though I had twenty years of experience working with children through the foster care system, none of the children that I had fostered prepared me for what I encountered with this young woman.

She had gone through a series of abusive situations and lived in a constant battle for her life. No matter how much I reached out to her, she would not let me get close. It pained me to see her struggling daily and not be able to help with her hurt. I knew God desperately wanted her to know and experience His love, but I did not know how to get through to her. As I prayed and asked God to give me wisdom about how I could be a mother to her, He began to show me that it was not my motherly instincts that were motivating me, but a codependency problem that I was not aware of at that time. I found out that when you are codependent, you think that a person needs you. Instead of being a helper, you end up being a hindrance.

As I began to read and understand more about

codependency, I realized that this young teenager needed my love and not my pity. Through this trial, I was able to love and listen to her heart when she was down. I can go on and on about how this one child changed my life through each test that was designed for me. If God had not given me the wisdom I needed, I would have blamed her for the struggles we were going through. He was testing my faith to trust Him for this child that He brought into my life to be a blessing to me.

By God's wisdom, I was able to become the kind of mother she needed, firm in discipline, yet gentle in heart, able to give godly direction without hindering her from walking in the victory God desired for her life. As our relationship finally deepened, I thought I had come to the turning point in my relationship with this young girl. Like Katrina in the story at the beginning of this chapter, God was actually drawing me to a closer relationship with Him. God was not only testing my faith and developing the love and patience I needed to endure with her during that season of her life, but He also revealed some deep-rooted issues inside of me that needed to be healed.

After God exposed my own inadequacies, it was evident to me that I needed the working of the Holy Spirit in my life. Nevertheless, in spite of my own shortcomings, God honored my prayers according to His word, and filled my empty cup with everything I needed to accomplish the task:

> *"Grace and peace be multiplied to you in the knowledge of God and of Jesus our Lord, as His divine power has given to us all things that pertain to life and godliness, through the knowledge of Him who called us by glory and virtue."*
> *(2 Peter 1:2)*

God's Word says that in the knowledge of God and of Jesus our Lord, grace and peace will be multiplied to us. In other words, we will have an abundance of wisdom in the things of God. It is wonderful to know that our knowledge—or lack thereof—does not determine whether or not God can use us. God uses us at His discretion and out of His loving kindness and wisdom; He pours the Holy Spirit inside of us, providing what we need to do His work.

The Helper Who Guides Us to All Truths

God gives us wisdom, but the Holy Spirit leads us in the right direction to receive the wisdom needed to have peace in the midst of any situation. In John 14:26-27, Jesus encouraged his disciples in saying:

> *"But the Helper, the Holy Spirit, whom the Father will send in My name, He will teach you all things, and bring to your remembrance all things that I said to you. Peace I leave with you. My peace I give to you; not as the world gives do I give to you. Let not your heart be troubled, neither let it be afraid."*

That is good news! You and I do not have to do the will of God in our own wisdom. We have the Holy Spirit as our teacher and guide. Jesus saw the need to encourage His disciples in yet another scripture: *"However, when He, the Spirit of truth, has come, He will guide you into all truth; for He will not speak on His own authority, but whatever he hears He will speak; and He will tell you things to come." (John 16:13)*

Pursuing God's peace is done through prayer. In every season of our lives, we need to seek God's peace by asking the Holy Spirit for wisdom in every situation. When we ask the Holy Spirit for wisdom, He leads us to Jesus so we can walk in peace. I believe that in return, Jesus leads us into a place of rest. There is a difference between peace and rest. Rest is a place where God wants to take us. Jesus tells us to come to Him, a place of abiding in Him, and He will give us rest. When we give our burdens to Jesus, His yoke is easy and the burden is light. We cannot carry this load, we must give it to Him, and then we can be still and know that He is God.

I thank God that He gave us the Holy Spirit to help us walk in all truth. We need God to open our hearts and ears so that we can hear clearly what the Holy Spirit is saying to us concerning every circumstance. Then, after we have prayed, we need to rest in God with the confidence that in our day-to-day battles, we have the victory.

My Prayer

Lord, I need your wisdom. You said if I ask for wisdom, you would give it to me freely. I stand before Your throne of grace and ask for an infilling of Your wisdom. I need Your Holy Spirit to stretch and strengthen my faith without fear of being out of Your will for my life. The only way I can walk with divine power in obedience and discipline throughout every area of my life is by Your Holy Spirit. I admit, I need You to teach and guide me into all truth.

Therefore, I will wait on You, Holy Spirit, to fill me with the wisdom I need to rest in You. Oh Lord, how comforting it is to know that You care about everything I do on a daily basis. Thank You for Your peace, which is available to me through Your Son, Jesus Christ. I will diligently pursue Your peace by not complaining about the road You choose to have me travel in order to receive Your wonderful promises. I can rest in those promises. Oh Lord, with great joy and delight, I am excited about You all over again!

What Is The View from Your Window?

1. Do you practice asking God for wisdom in your daily life when you are going through testing and trials? How can asking for wisdom help you strengthen your faith?

2. How often do you search the Word of God for wisdom for every situation of your life? Ask the Holy Spirit to help you understand His Word. Every day, get a Bible, pen, tablet, and dictionary, and begin to go to the Holy Spirit School.

3. In this season of your life, stop and thank God for your growth and for giving you wisdom in each trial.

CHAPTER FIVE
The Season of Abiding in Christ

"As the Father loved Me, I also have loved you;
Abide in My Love."
(John 15:9)

I can remember the season in my marriage when I was learning how to abide in Christ. I look back at that period and can still envision the pruning process that began in a small closet. As a teenager and young adult, I was very popular in school and involved with the social groups. I was driven by my own ambitions and strongly believed that as long as I had me, there was no stopping success from manifesting itself in my life. Confident in myself, I never depended on others to make me and was never threatened by anyone else's ability to break me.

You can imagine the hardship I faced after I was saved and God began to strip me of my old self to make me a new creature. *"Therefore if any man be in Christ, he is a new creature, old things are passed away behold all things are become new." (II Corinthians 5:17)* Not long after my college years, I was married and settled down. Then a year after my husband and I exchanged wedding vows, we accepted Jesus Christ as our Lord and Savior and made a decision to serve Him. Salvation came immediately, but sanctification was a much longer process.

For as long as I could remember, I had always functioned in a position of power: star athlete on the track team, cheerleader, and president of the class. Therefore, I packed all of my credentials and trophies in my baggage as a reminder of who I was. I began to walk in my new role as a wife and a Christian; I realized there was little room in my future for my past successes. God wanted to do a new thing!

Each day was spent trying to be all that my husband demanded, but I could not measure up to the image of the perfect wife that I thought I was supposed to be. For the first time in my life, I was no match for the opponent. I felt like a failure, but I learned to hide my discontentment behind a mask. However, it was not long before the persistent demands from my husband overwhelmed me and caused my mask to become tattered and disfigured. The battle with my husband was constant and so was the raging war within me. Finally, I came to a place of brokenness and remembered the Lord.

In My Secret Place

Daily I would secretly meet with God in my bedroom closet. Often, our meeting was without words, just salty tears and a contrite heart. I wanted so much for God to change my situation, but He did the very opposite. He changed me! In my time with the Lord, I would receive specific instructions on what to do concerning my husband. Out of my love for God, I obeyed His word. It took some time, but eventually I began to see God's hand move in my marriage. Like David, my soul began to thirst for God, stirring my heart's desire to seek after Him each day. I learned through God's Word that in order for me to survive, I had to surrender the old me, and abide (or remain) in God so that He could change me.

> *"I am the true vine, and My Father is the vinedresser. Every branch in Me that does not bear fruit He takes away and every branch that bears fruit He prunes, that it may bear more fruit. You are already clean because of the word,*

> which I have spoken to you. Abide in
> Me, and I in you. As the branch cannot
> bear fruit of itself, unless it abides in
> the vine, neither can you, unless you
> abide in Me." (John 15:1-4)

Through my thirst for Him, I learned to abide in a place I never knew before. I began to find out that I could not do anything if I did not abide in His presence and eat of His word.

Changing My Way of Thinking

We must acknowledge our self-worth in Christ Jesus and not compare ourselves to the world's criteria of being valuable. If we do not, we will have a difficult time letting go of the old self so that we can embrace the new man God has formed us to be. Being a new creature in Christ requires you to do more than just declare it. You must also think it by renewing your mind (Rom. 12:2), and walk it out by abiding in Christ.

> "If indeed you have heard Him and
> have been taught by Him, as the truth is
> in Jesus. That you put off, concerning
> your former conduct, the old man
> which grows corrupt according to the
> deceitful lusts, and be renewed in the
> spirit of your mind and that you put on
> the new man which was created
> according to God, in true righteousness
> and holiness." (Ephesians 21-24)

Renewing your mind is not a suggestion but a commandment for life. If you do not renew your mind, you will not be able to see yourself as anything other than the way in which you have always seen yourself. When you renew your mind and abide in Christ, you are able to take off the old clothes and put on the new. Little by little, through His word, God will strip away the old and clothe you in garments of righteousness. As part of our inheritance as sons and daughters of God, we have the assurance that God will fulfill His promises concerning us. Since we know that God cannot lie, we can have confidence that He will do His part. Because we have a part to do, too, once we have been cleansed and given new clothes, we should no longer desire to wear our old clothes anymore.

A Change of Clothing

I can remember the excitement I felt whenever the new school year started. My excitement was not for class, but the clothes. You see, each school year my mother would take us shopping for new clothes. I think my eyes were big as silver dollars when I saw all the colors and different styles; I wanted one of everything. At that time, my mother had to buy for seven children, so we were limited as to what we could have. In spite of our economic status, I thought I was rich in my new clothes. Some of the children would wait a few weeks into the school year before they wore their new clothes. Not me! By the end of the first week of school, I had already worn everything new she had bought me. Once I ran out of my new clothes, I dreaded the idea of having to wear my old stuff again.

As Christians, we should exhibit that same type of excitement concerning the new garments that Jesus' blood bought for us. By reading the Word of God, renewing our minds, and abiding in Christ, we are able to put on the new man. Unfortunately, too many of us have access to this brand new wardrobe, but are waiting to put it on. Instead, we are weighted down unnecessarily by our old nature: anger, contention, jealousy, hated, unforgiveness, fornication, adultery, and idolatry.

The old nature can keep us living beneath what God intended for us, because we do not understand who we are in Christ. Our old self remains a slave to the past when we reject Christ, and the devil knows it. This is why the enemy wants us to live in denial and stay silent about our past failures so that he can quietly torment us with memories of the shame and embarrassment. The enemy understands that if we come into the knowledge of who we are in Christ, we would prosper in the things of God. He knows that we are children of the most High God, and that God wants to give us an inheritance. He is willing to do everything he can to try to stop that from happening.

Our Spiritual Blessings

The good news, according to Ephesians 1:3, is that we have access to every spiritual blessing that is in the Kingdom of God! *"Blessed be the God and Father of our Lord Jesus Christ, who has blessed us with every spiritual blessing in the heavenly places in Christ."* It is so important that we know what blessings and promises we have in Jesus. These spiritual blessings are ours to claim: His redemption, being chosen, holiness, forgiveness, inheritance, and knowledge. I can say in my heart, "I am a new creature, free in Christ Jesus, and I have access to the Father." We must realize that we have all these blessings and much more in Christ Jesus. God wants to prune us from our old nature so that we can fully experience His promises and blessings.

Did you know that God never intended for sin to have dominion over us? He designed us for fellowship with

Him; because of sin, we have fallen out of relationship with God. This is why Christ died for us, rose again and is sitting at the right hand of the Father daily making intercession for us, so that we can be forgiven of our sins, restored to our original purpose, and live a life pleasing unto God. The hard part has already been done. Jesus has already defeated the devil, taken back the keys, and has set us free from the bondages of sin.

How do we let go of the past? Once we have made the decision, then God will help us each step of the way. He even promises to provide a way of escape when temptation comes *(see 1 Corinthians 10:13)*. We must be willing to let go of those things that keep us living in the past: old friends, relationships, worldly music, certain television shows and movies, gossiping, lying: anything representing ungodliness.

God wants to lead you out of the things that are unholy so that you can live a life that is holy. He is ready to bring you out of the wilderness and its vicious cycle of sin and into the Promised Land flowing with milk and honey! In *John 14:16-21*, Jesus is speaking about the love relationship between Him and believers. He recognizes that we will struggle, walking in obedience to Him, so He prays that our Father would send us a Helper, the Holy Spirit, who will abide with us forever. God has put His Spirit inside of us to dwell and help us to walk in victory in every area of our lives. The Holy Spirit convicts us when we are in sin, and Jesus stands ready to prune our hearts so that we can bear much fruit. He needs our permission to do it, just as a doctor needs our permission to operate on us.

Spiritual Surgery

Have you ever thought about how easily we trust a

doctor, his prognosis, judgment and abilities in the operating room, yet have difficulty trusting Jesus, the One who died out of an unconditional love for us? Jesus truly has our best interest at heart, which is why He gives us His Word as our prescription for abiding in abundant living.

In *John 15:4*, Jesus tells us to abide in Him. To abide means to stay, be still, and rest in Him. We need to yield ourselves totally to Him so we can hear God speak. When I made the decision to give myself totally to God, I had no clue of the disease of sin that was still festering inside of me. Once He gave me the diagnosis, I knew I needed Him to prune my heart and bring clarity to the confusion in my life.

Every morning I set aside time to meet Him. In order for Him to do the work, I needed to make an effort to show up. I did not always know exactly what to say to Him, so I would pray and ask, "Lord what is it? What do I do next?" In the quiet place where it appeared I was alone, I oftentimes wondered if God was even listening. I sat still and waited as patiently as I could, warm tears streaming down my face. Somehow, He always managed to comfort me with His word, and my heart would overflow with high expectations that something wonderful was going to happen.

It was difficult at first to just sit there and wait because I have a very active mind and lifestyle. After awhile, I disciplined my mind from wandering about the cares of the day, and learned to be still and rest in knowing that He is God. Instead of going over my "to-do" list in my mind, I meditated on praise songs and the praise words in the book of Psalms. These times were wonderful, because the Master was doing surgery on my heart, and I was resting in His hands.

God was always faithful to wield His Word in my

circumstances and comfort me at the same time. I knew the most effective way of hearing from God was through His Word, so I kept a pen, journal, and Bible next to me every morning. Without fail, God would bring me to a scripture that directly related to areas in my nature that needed to be healed; facing my insecurities, the way I spoke to people, my selfish behavior, or my attitude toward my husband. No matter the underlying factor, I always found myself repenting to God and to those I had hurt. Repentance is the medicine that brings forth the healing. If you are honest with yourself, you will see that repentance is the kind of medicine prescribed to *take daily as needed*. It probably will not taste good, but it is good for you.

The issues that I faced then are not the same matters of the heart that God is dealing with me about today. However, I honestly believe that if I had stopped the pruning process because it seemed too difficult to press my way through, I would still be carrying around the same baggage from my past. My deliverance was a combination of my determination and desire to be set free; God's grace and faithfulness to His promises concerning me; and the effective, fervent prayers of my sister, who prayed continually for me.

The process is very similar to surgery. God searches your heart, reviews the X-rays (deep-rooted issues are oftentimes unseen by the naked eye), gives you the diagnosis, and then discusses the need for surgery to correct the problem. Your job is to sign the permission papers, show up for the operation, and follow His instructions during the recovery process. Once we have given the Holy Spirit permission to do surgery on us, we must then take our place on the operating table of trust and allow the Doctor to begin His work.

The Holy Spirit is the doctor in the surgery room of

our hearts, and He knows exactly what "cancer" to cut away so that we can experience a full and abundant life. Cancer is a malignant evil that corrodes slowly and fatally. If we were diagnosed with cancer in the natural, we would be anxious for treatment, hopeful for a full recovery, and willing to do exactly as instructed. We should have the same desire for healing in our spiritual man, who is slowly dying by the "cancers" of bitterness and pride.

Have you ever considered how quickly we go to the doctor when we are not feeling our normal selves? We trust the diagnosis and take the medication he or she prescribes. After all, doctors must know what they are doing, they have a degree! We trust a doctor's knowledge, skills, and judgment, because we assume he knows what he is doing and is qualified for the job. If we can trust a man or woman this way, how much more can we trust the One who created us, loves us, and gave His only begotten Son for our sake?

As with any doctor, it is imperative that we follow instructions so that our time of recovery can progress smoothly. If you are accustomed to doing everything for yourself, you are going to appreciate the fact that in this, you do not have to do anything. God will do all the work. You just need to yield yourself totally to Him, so you can hear the Holy Spirit and be willing to follow Him.

I can still remember the day I decided to give myself totally to God, so He could take the cancer out of my life. I had no clue as to what to expect. I did know I needed Him to fix my heart and work on areas of my life that were tied into knots by lack of wisdom, confusion, and hurt.

Going Through the Healing Process

In my time of waiting, God was always faithful to

speak to me through His Word. I knew this was the most effective way to hear from God, so I always kept a pen, journal, and Bible next to me every morning. God would always lead me to scriptures that clarified the "cancer" in my life: how my selfishness and past insecurities were ordering my footsteps, instead of His Word. I found myself constantly repenting to Him and seeing the need to repent to others. My healing process had begun.

Though repentance is the medicine that brings forth healing, it is not easy to swallow. As Christians, we cannot expect forgiveness from God or others unless we exercise our obligation to repent for our sins. Repentance, like the advertisement for milk, does our body good!

Your process of healing may not be exactly what I encountered, but the same principles outlined below should apply:

- **Ask the Holy Spirit for help!** *(John 14:26):* We must first ask the Holy Spirit to open our hearts and reveal that which is in us that is not pleasing to God. In essence, we are asking Him to reveal the disease that keeps us from experiencing a strong, healthy life in God. In Jeremiah 17:9 it says, "The heart is deceitful above all things, and desperately wicked; who can know it?" Since we do not know our own hearts, we need the help of Holy Spirit to give us revelation of deep-rooted sins.

- **Prepare to hear from Him** *(Psalms 27:4- 8):* In many of today's classrooms, small, hand-held tape recorders have replaced the old-fashioned pen and paper method of taking notes. Regardless of the technique used for gaining knowledge, we do what works for us to remember what we need so that we may pass the course. We should make the same investment when we go into the Presence of the Lord. We should expect to hear something of great importance from God and be prepared to take notes on what He is speaking to us through His Word.

- **Be quiet and still** *(Psalm 46:10):* We do not like being still, because we see our value in doing things so that we can become somebody in life. We live in a fast-paced world, and our objective is to keep up and take the lead whenever possible.

- **Trust God** *(Psalms 37:3-5):* Learn to trust Him by faith and share your most intimate thoughts, fears, and hurts with Him. Jesus is your friend, and He wants you to be able to talk to Him about anything that concerns you.

- **Renew your mind** *(Romans 12:2):* Let Him take you back to your past for a moment so that you can understand why you are the way you are. He does not want to remind you of your old self to spite you; He takes you back so that He can deliver you and remove the chains of shame and embarrassment that keep you from going forward.

- **Repent and Forgive** *(Matt. 5:23-26):* This is a time to forgive and repent of things you have done, even those things you were not aware of. You may have hidden anger in your heart towards your husband, children, or a friend. Whomever you are angry with, God will reveal it, even if it is toward Him. If you find out that the root of your anger lies with God because you have blamed Him for the things you suffered in your past, talk it out with

God. He already knows how you feel. He wants you to bring your issues with Him to Him so that He can give you understanding. God deeply cares for you, and He does not want sin to have dominion over your life. Sin separates you from God; repentance brings you back into fellowship with Him.

- **Meet Him every day** *(John 15:4-5):* We want to please our flesh by allowing other things to take the place of our time with God. We get busy with life and try to fit God into our schedule.

- **Be accountable** *(James 5:16):* Make yourself accountable to someone who is mature, such as your Pastor and his wife, a leader in your Church, or a wise woman. He gave us each other to help us grow and overcome with victory every area of our lives. If you have a problem finding or trusting someone with whom to be accountable, pray and ask God to help you. It is not God's intention for you to bear your burdens alone.

- **Do not stop the process!** *(Psalms 24:4-7):* Sometimes we stop the process because it hurts, and we want the pain to go away. It may seem as though the Holy Spirit is against us because He reminds us of the things we do not want to remember. However, that is not true. Going back is a part of the healing process, so that we may go forward. If we stop the process, our suffering in the end will be much greater than our current afflictions. Just as we are unable to get up from the operating table during surgery, we should lie still on God's pruning table until He has finished His work in us.

- **Abide in Him** *(John 15:1-4):* Failure to yield to any principle mentioned above could hinder or stop the pruning and healing process. When we stop abiding and seeking the Lord, we take the health of our hearts into our own hands and risk further injury.

We have Jesus the Son, God the Father, and the Holy Spirit dwelling in our temples, helping us with each of these principles. He has given us His Word that He will never leave nor forsake us. He will be right there, helping us grow from glory to glory. It is a wonderful thought that God wants to prune and heal us so He can dwell in us. Oh, how glorious the thought of having our Father dwelling with us on a daily basis.

The pruning and healing process will help you to identify who you are in Christ, and to develop the fruits of love, peace, joy, goodness, kindness, long suffering, faithfulness, self-control, and patience you need in your Christian walk. Which of the fruit of the Spirit do you lack? Are you growing in each one of these areas? How can you have control over your temper, eating habits, and patience with others? How can you love your spouse, children, and others more? Where is your peace and joy? Jesus wants to develop all of His fruit in you, and He is waiting on you to give Him your permission by simply saying, "Lord, I'm ready to get to know You, and who I am in You."

My Prayer

Father, thank you for teaching me how to abide in you each day. I pray that you continue to prune me and take me through the healing process. I need you, Holy Spirit, to take out the areas in my life that are not pleasing to God. I desire to bear the fruit of You, Lord, but it can be so hard to love when someone does not love you. I want to remain in your love and Word, so I can learn to love as you love. I want the garments of past to be stripped off me, so I can walk in the newness of Your Word. I know this will take time, and I must yield my life totally to You. Lord, help me when I am weak. I need your strength in order to continue on during those days when I feel like I cannot make it. Lord, I am ready for you to develop your fruit that I so desperately need in my walk with you.

What is The View from Your Window?

1. Do you find yourself having a hard time persevering through the difficult times of your life? Write a note to God, and ask Him to help you to abide with Him as He develops the fruit of the Holy Spirit in your heart.

2. What are some of the things you can do to change the way you think as you abide in Christ? Let Him take the cancer of hurt, bitterness, unforgiveness, and abuse out of your heart.

3. Stop and confess to the Lord His Word by speaking His blessing and promises: You are spiritually blessed, redeemed, chosen for holiness, forgiven, and I am His special child. Read Ephesians Chapters 1-3 and continue to proclaim His promises.

CHAPTER SIX
The Season of Intimacy

I am my beloved's, and his desire is toward me.
(Song of Solomon 7:10

The smell of rain fills the air, and a gentle breeze caresses the evening; somehow, you know that spring has sprung. The sun unfolds the budding flowers that have waited patiently to become beautiful blooms, emitting bouquets of fragrances. A drive through a botanical garden this time of the year can be simply breathtaking. Without even realizing it, you have stood by to watch bumblebees pollinate, and birds return to their nest. There is an excitement that comes with spring, expectancy that intimacy and love will bloom. The season of intimacy reminds me of the spring. Like flowers, we, too, have the capability to blossom while basking in the Son. Imagine the fresh drizzling rain of the Holy Spirit quenching our barrenness and refreshing our soul. Is not love grand?

In this chapter, we will not only hear of the love and passion Jesus has for us, but also see it as He draws us into His chambers. Jesus wants a personal and loving relationship with us, but in order for us to receive it; we must discipline ourselves through submission and spend time in His Presence. It is evident just how passionate our Father feels about us when we allow the Holy Spirit to reveal the heart of God to us.

Jesus desires to quench our thirst for Him through our acceptance of Him in our lives. He said in *John 7:38-39, "If anyone thirsts, let him come to Me and drink."* This is an invitation from Christ for anyone willing to surrender his or her empty life for a full life through Christ. When we come to Christ and drink of Him, He promises to fill us with the Holy Spirit, the river of living water. For many, the idea of becoming a Christian means being bound up or enjoying only a limited measure of life. In all actuality, there is more freedom in Christ than outside of Him. In Christ, there is joy unspeakable, but apart from Him, one can only expect to experience happiness, which is based on something good happening in our lives.

Real love is freedom, not bondage. In Christ, we can anticipate His arms of unconditional love embracing us, in spite of our shortcomings, appearance, or income. Jesus wants us to come into an intimate, heart-to-heart, face-to-face relationship with Him. He shows us His passion; His desire is to be intimate with us, and that He becomes the love of our lives. His Word encourages and builds us, as it removes the barriers of old areas of insecurities and loneliness. The Lord wants to teach us how to embrace His love, and how we should love each other.

A Weekend of Intimacy

One of the most intimate moments I ever experienced with my husband was when we went away for a weekend to spend some quiet time together away from the busyness of work, family, and ministry. I had been praying to the Lord and asking Him to teach me how to love my husband. I never imagined that it could be so wonderful. That weekend, my husband and I spent a great deal of time sharing intimately with one another our hearts, thoughts, fears, and dreams. At some point in our being transparent and honest, the Lord placed it on my heart to ask my husband if he would allow me to wash his feet. He looked deeply into my eyes and answered yes.

My husband sat in a huge, comfortable chair, while I took a very vulnerable and humbling position on the floor at his feet. With the warm water from my pail, I began to wash his feet. I still remember how a gamut of emotions flooded my heart as I looked up at my husband with tears streaming down my face. In a loving tone, he asked me, "Why are you crying?" My heart was full of words but my mouth would not speak them. I swallowed hard and managed to quietly say, "I love you so much."

The experience was simply priceless, and God's presence was obvious. I wept, knowing that I was in the Lord's chambers, and as I washed my husband's feet, the Lord was washing me with His love. I wanted to stay right there for the rest of the night. I was so taken in by my husband, and how different he looked to me that night, that I gave in to my heart and fell deeply in love with him.

That weekend is a reminder to me that we must stop in our busy lives and spend time seeking the face of the Lover of our heart. God can be found when we seek Him with diligence. In *Proverbs 8:17*, it says, *"I love those who love me, and those who seek me diligently will find me."*

In that one evening, I found a place in my husband's heart that had never been revealed to me before. However, it required me to submit to the will of God by taking a lowly position, and trusting God to cover me in His love. I learned that a woman could honor God through her faith in Him, and by her submission to Him without feeling less valuable because she is a woman.

Through an intimate relationship with God, a woman can understand why she was created and can appreciate her role in life. If a woman does not understand her womanhood and why God made her a woman, she may become resentful and fight against God's plan in order to try to prove her equality to man.

No matter what position a woman holds, it was never God's intention for her to take on the responsibilities given to man. We can see that in Genesis when God punished Adam and Eve for their sin. The consequences were equally shared, but the specifics of their consequences were distinctly different.

The key to intimacy is submission. Too often, we submit ourselves to everything and everyone else, except God. It is not until all else fails that we turn to Him in desperate times, in need of receiving His saving power. When we embrace submission, we also embrace the discipline needed to be successful in our journey with the Lord. Scripture tells us in *James 4:7, "Therefore, submit to God, resist the devil and he will flee from you. Draw near to God and He will draw near to you."* When we cease fighting God, submit to Him in heart and deed, and rest in His covering, we allow Jesus to walk us through every situation victoriously, taking us from glory to glory.

In the Love Chambers with Jesus

If you did not catch it earlier, let me take a more subtle approach to point this out—when you sow submission, you will reap a great reward. When I submitted to God and sowed into my marriage by washing my husband's feet, I reaped a great reward: entrance into the love chambers with Jesus. Submission to His love causes me to embrace the discipline necessary to come into His chambers and change my life. I love the way Jesus takes us into the love chambers of His heart. That moment with my husband was a time I will always cherish. My love for him still overflows with excitement. However, I must say my time spent with the Lord explodes with excitement as He whispers words of His love in my ear.

I can remember a season of passion as the Lord was sharing with me how to come into His love chambers. As I meditated on His Word in the Song of Solomon, He began to lead me into His chambers that day. With His loving heart, He gently led me into a secret, quiet place where He wanted to share His affection. The presence of His love filled the room as the words from Song of Solomon began to come off the page into my heart. Those words were like a song to me in the air, dancing into my heart as He spoke them to me. Gazing into His eyes as He spoke those words of adoration, they began to affirm me in my heart. The words of affirmation drew me closer into His presence and worship flooded my heart for Him. The words of Jesus began to speak to me. He said, *"Daughter you are the apple of my eye, and I have given you so much favor and grace. Now walk with Me in My grace, Dolores, I have given it to you so freely."* At that moment, as those words of adoration began to affirm me, I felt that freedom in my heart as we continued our walk together through His Word.

As time passed, we continued to flow in the river of love. As I sat in His presence, I felt so naked before Him, but for some reason, I felt no shame, as He covered me with His love. Whenever we are willing to expose the truth of who we are, we take away the camouflage that hides us, and then the Lord can provide the right kind of covering that protects us. And that is exactly what the Lord did for me; He covered me with the garment of His love.

He revealed to me that it was not my outward appearance that captured His breath, but my inward Spirit that He delighted in. He began to say to me in a gentle way, *"Daughter, I love you the way you are and not by what I see outwardly. I am looking at your heart, and I see My princess."* The beauty He saw in me amazed me, because I did not see myself to be beautiful the way He saw me. As I sat quietly, the sweet Holy Spirit began to strengthen and fill me with His love.

What was happening to me? Never had I ever felt this

way about the Lord, even though He told us in His Word that His Spirit will strengthen us in our inner man and Christ will dwell in our hearts through faith, that we could be rooted and grounded in His love. He wanted me to know His love that passes knowledge, and to fill me with the fullness of God, according to His Word. (*Ephesians 3:16-19*). Moments passed as I was drinking from the river of His love, which was overwhelming to my soul. All the while, I could hear myself saying, *"Lord, I cannot handle such love that you are expressing to me."* I wanted more, but I could not contain it as I sat there in His awesome presence, weeping. Somehow time was not important, as I lay, awake on the floor, staring and waiting for Jesus' next move. I began to feel so much freedom in His love chambers. There was freedom from insecurities, hurt, abuse, shame, and worries. So much freedom was there, that I could not explain how free my heartfelt, to love without boundaries and bondages. We struggle with loving others because of our walls and bondages of the past. However, as we seek Jesus in His love chambers, He takes away the hurt and pain so we can freely love as He loves us.

Each moment was special to me, as He looked into my eyes. There we were together, longing to be with each other. This reminded me of that week-end with my husband, standing face to face, with moments of passion, and lost for words. The world stops in this moment of love and facing each other. Imagine being face-to-face and breath-to-breath with God! The passion of that experience left me lost for words. However, the psalmist wonderfully expresses the attitude of my heart toward the Lord: the word says, *"...in the secret place of His tabernacle He shall hide me...",* and when He said, *"Seek My face,"* my heart said, *"Your face, Lord, I will seek; do not hide Your face from me." (Psalm 27:6)*

Through His loving presence and the whispers of His words, I could hear Him say, *"I am pleased with you."* Once again, through those affirming words, He was reminding me that it is my heart that that He was looking at, and He knew the love I had for Him. I will always remember those words coming from Him as He spoke into the depths of my heart, *"Dolores, you love Me so much. I know the love you have for me."* I did not have words to say at that moment; only tears of joy streaming down my face.

Those words were so valuable and precious to me because I did not know my own heart. When I heard Him say to me what was in my heart, I was taken by those words. I did not know my love for Him was so evident to Him. Jeremiah tells us that the heart is deceitful and wicked. *(Jeremiah 17:9)* Yet, with all of the passion that filled that room, I kept wondering how could I love someone like God, who is the very essence of love, when I knew in my soul that there was nothing good in me. Only the Lord could search my heart and share with me what was dwelling in it.

At that moment, I was surrounded by a river of water much deeper than I could handle. With His arms extended out, He was asking me to come into the deeper parts of the water. I was hesitant, because I felt safe and secure where I was in this moment of our love. Fears began to settle in my heart, because I knew I could not swim. I whispered those words to Him; *"Lord, I do not know how to swim,"* as if He did not know my fears. In response to my excuses, He said, *"Come Dolores, I would carry you to the next place in My love chambers. Come into the deeper parts of the river of love, and you will find My love that will overflow your heart in this place. Come, daughter."*

As He beckoned me to come closer with a soft-spoken voice, He said, *"I will be with you, I will not forsake you."* Fear gripped my heart and I could not find the courage to completely let go of me and lunge into deep. I had to let go of my fears and step out on faith, and trust His love for me, but still hesitant to walk further, I began to take baby steps toward Him. The closer I got to Him, the more I could tell the water was warm and inviting. My heart began to long for more of what He had waiting for me in the deeper part of the river. I was not thinking anymore of what might happen; I was drawn in by His love that was pulling me closer to Him. I was out there, overtaken by the river, and the water was over my head. However, I felt so safe and secure in His arms as He held me, assuring me He would never let me go. I was so close as I embraced the Lord's love for me. I only wanted more of what He had waiting for me in the deeper part of the river.

Lost in the deep river of love, where I had forgotten I could not swim, I clung tightly to His promise that He would never let me go. After a while, I found myself lying there in such a rest that overtook me as time passed slowly. This place was so peaceful that I found myself sound asleep. When I awoke, the fragrance of His presence, and the memory of the river were still warm in my heart. The thoughts of being in His presence overwhelmed my heart.

When we stop to seek Him, there is such a rest in His secret place. In His chambers, we will find words of adoration and love that are so valuable to the soul. The intimate words in Songs of Solomon chapter seven came to build and fill us up with His love, joy, and peace. Go into the love chamber of God and you will never be the same.

The Heart of Jesus in Song of Solomon

I can share with you many moments of intimacy with Jesus, but I want you to develop your own moments with the Lord by spending precious time with Him alone. As I began to meditate on the Song of Solomon, chapter seven, my heart was melted by the words. Stop for a moment and let the Holy Spirit show you the heart of Jesus in Song of Solomon, chapter seven, as He speaks passionate words of love to you by adorning you from the bottom of your feet to the top of your head. Jesus says, "*...you are a princess, and your feet are graceful in their sandals, your thighs are work of art, each one a jewel; the work of the hands of a skillful workman." (Song of Solomon 7:1)* The word "princess" is a female member of a royal family. We are royalty with our King and He values our relationship with Him and the Father. He has given us grace and favor to walk as His royal priesthood. Hear the words of Jesus as He whispers in your ear in those intimate times spent with Him... *"You are a princess, the apple of My eye. You are beautiful, and your feet are graceful in their sandals."* Our feet in sandals are a symbol of occupancy, possession, the act of taking possession, as of a property. He loves it when we walk in His grace and not our own prideful will, because He gives grace to the humble and resists the proud. He loves giving us favor and supplying us with the abundance of His love.

As we continue to flow in this river of love, He continues with words of love and adoration. *"Your navel is a wine glass filled to overflowing. Your body is full and slender like a bundle of wheat bound together. He looks at the fullness of our body and knows it needs to be filled with Him. (Song of Solomon 7:2)* This is the place in our body (or the Body of Christ) that holds His love and anointing. We want the infilling of Holy Spirit to fill us so we can walk in the overflow of His love. We want to know the love of Christ, which passes knowledge; that we may be filled with all the fullness of God.

The beauty of our breast is that it brings pleasure and

freedom to our relationship. Gazelles are does, or young deer, that were never meant o be tamed. They belong in the wild, following their own inner laws of joyous, unbounded freedom. The Lord looks at our wonderful breasts and sees the freedom He has given us to please Him. He never intended us to be in bondage to the idols we had in our past. Now you are free, and that freedom brings forth joy. *"I charge you, O daughters of Jerusalem, By the gazelles or by the does of the field, do not stir up nor awaken my love until it pleases. (Song of Solomon 7:3)* He has given us freedom to love with an unconditional love, but only through Jesus can we love with a love that is not conditional. We are stirred in our hearts to love without the bondage of our own baggage. We are free at last, and we are free indeed.

He looks into our eyes and whispers to us saying: *"Your neck is like ivory, and your eyes sparkle like the pools of Heshbon by the gate of Bahh-Rabbim. Your nose is beautiful like Mount Lebanon." (Song of Solomon 7:4)* The tower of Lebanon was a famous and beautiful projecting tower in an unspecified city near the eastern slopes of Hermon. As you stand straight before Him, He looks into the beauty of your eyes, and touching your face, as He sees how radiant and beautiful it is from your neck to your nose to your eyes. He desires for us to rise early and seek His face. How intimate our relationship with Jesus can be when we see Him face to face. We had a time of intimacy that was face to face. *"When You said, seek My face," my heart said to You, Your face, Lord I will seek. (Psalms 27:8-9)*

To seek means to diligently look for, to search earnestly until the object of the search is located. We must stop in our busy lives and spend time seeking the face of God. Just as I found a place in my husband's heart I never saw before, something I had been seeking in our relationship for years; nevertheless, it was not until that one special time that I found the treasure I had been digging deeply for. We must be diligent in our seeking, not giving up, because He can be found.

I can feel Him lifting my head up and telling me, *"Your head is held high like Mount Carmel; your hair is so lovely, it holds a king prisoner."* Now that I am communing with Him, it brings me into a place of faith and confidence. When we walk in fellowship with God, we walk in faith and confidence. Our head is lifted up high, because we know who we are in Christ. He assures and anchors us in His love so we can walk in confidence. Then, we can say we have been rooted and grounded in His love. When the Lord speaks of our hair, He refers to it as our covering. We can understand more about the importance of our hair in *I Corinthian 11:15, "But if a woman has long hair, it is a glory to her; for her hair is given to her for a covering."* (Also see *Song of Solomon 7:5.*)

When a woman can submit herself to the covering God has chosen for her and walk in quietness, she is captured by such love for Him. What He teaches her as a woman, is that she can be confident of who she is in Him. She does not feel diminished, or that it is not fair to be a woman. When we are covered in relationship with God, and our husband as the shepherd He has chosen for us, we can walk with Jesus from glory to glory. He is pleased, and taken by our love for Him through obedience to His word. We must be women of integrity, who know how to build up and not tear down. This pleases God, when we give ourselves over to His direction for our lives.

I just love it when God tells me I am beautiful and desirable. Why is it that we that do not see the beauty God sees in us? The word "beauty" means the quality of being very pleasing, as in form. Being pleasing to God is not in the outward form, as the world has instilled inside of our minds, which keeps us in bondage to the world's point of view. God tells us in His word that He does not look at the outward; He looks at the heart. When He looks into our heart, He only sees our beauty. We must reflect on the beauty that God sees in us, and not man. That helps us to continue to see our value in Him.

We are precious jewels to Him, that He cherishes. The Lord sees us as tall and slender, like a palm tree, and then He turns around and says that our breasts are full. A palm tree stands in a desert place, and it surrounded by wells of water. When He looks at you, He knows you are a well filled with His water, the Holy Spirit. This is how we bring comfort to others and Him. Breast-feeding is to bring forth food for a hungry and thirsty child. The entire chapter of *Isaiah 61* shows us that God desires to anoint us to help others. He said our breasts are full. We know as women that they are there to feed and please. In the latter part of verse three, He says, *"That they may be called trees of righteousness the planting of the Lord, that He may be glorified."* (Also see *Song of Solomon 7:8.*) We are His righteousness, and He has planted us in good soil that surrounds us with wells of water, so we can please and glorify Him.

He proceeds to climb that tree and cling to its branches. It is His desire to join us in oneness through our love affair of intimacy. Through this special time, it will draw us closer to Him. This is a place where nothing matters except being with Him. We love Him so much that we want to be obedient to His Word. When this happens, we become a dwelling place where we are able to abide in His everlasting love. He desires to kiss us with passionate love and embrace us as a prisoner. The word "kiss" is a sign of submission. When we kiss Him, we are embracing Jesus, to submit and trust only Him. We have a tendency to put our trust in everything else except God. *James 4:7-8* says: *"Therefore submit to God, Resist the devil and he will flee from you. Draw near to God and He will draw near to you."*

The word says how wonderful and tasty is a fruit of discipline; that is sweet to the Lord. When we allow Him to develop the fruit of the Spirit, we can please Him in every area of our lives. These words can be expressed in so many passionate ways. We can see the awesome love the King has for us through these scriptures. Just as Esther was required to be prepared to enter into an earthly king's chambers, we must be just as prepared for the Only King. How much more we must be prepared before we enter into the King of King's chambers. In Song of Solomon, chapter seven, in the first nine verses, the Lord loved on us from our feet to the top of our head. Now we should respond as in the last four verses to the One who has made covenant with us. Our love for Him should challenge Him to go with us to a place of intimacy and rest.

Responding to the Master

"Come, my beloved, let us go forth to the field and let us lodge in the villages." (Song of Solomon 7:11) Here, she desires to go into a place where they can show each other affection, the passion of love between the Lord and the one whom He loves so much. We can see their covenant relationship through the love affair that they have with each other. She recognizes that her relationship is secure and their passion for each other is mutual.

God desires this love affair to be just to the two of us together alone. He is a jealous God. He does not want us to put anything else before Him. He desires us for Himself. He loves us to be in a place of worship where we are alone with Him, in a place in His secret chambers, away from all the distractions that surround us on a daily basis. He desires our beauty of worship. Beauty, yophi (yohfee), means splendor, brightness, fairness, to be beautiful, lovely, fair, and graceful. He wants us, as women, to be beautiful in our hearts, faithful, loving, exciting in our passion of worship for Him. Listen to the passion in *Psalms 27:4*:

> *"I would love to be in His secret chambers, just the two of us, as we behold the beauty of each other in worship. I believe this scripture speaks for itself. We must have a desire to seek and spend intimate time with Him, and let Him hide us in that secret place of love."*

We must be in a place where we are connected to the vine, or we will not see the fruit. She desires to be in a place with Him so she can bear the fruit of His love. Notice two fruits that she mentions, grapes and pomegranates. Grapes produce the new wine in our lives. The new wine brings us fullness of His joy and pleasure. That pleasure brings the pomegranates into our lives. Pomegranate is a fruit that is bright and has plenty of seeds. Those seeds are the seeds of His love that He plants in us. With such passion, the Lord impregnates us with seeds of His love for Him and His people and with His vision for the lost. He wants us to reproduce who He is and spread this love to others. What an AWESOME GOD! This is a place where we desire to give Him our love and receive His love. *"The mandrakes give off a fragrance, and at our gates are pleasant fruits, all manner, new and old, which I have laid up for you, my beloved." (Song of Solomon 7:13)*

Mandrakes are plants that bear fruits that were thought to make you fertile. *Genesis 30:14-24* tells us a story where a woman was barren and desperate to have children. Rachel made a deal with Leah by telling Leah that she could be with her husband if Leah gives her mandrakes that Leah's son had given to her. Rachel is barren at this time, and she is desperate to have a baby. She puts her trust in other sources and not in God. The Word says, in verse twenty-two, *"Then God remembered Rachel, and God listened to her and opened her womb."* When we get in a desperate place in God, we must realize that no one can help us bear His fruit but Him. That word "remembered" means to visit. God visited Rachel and blessed her with a son. His vision and purpose was birthed out of desperation.

God desires us to be fertile, one who will reproduce Him to a dying world. He will open up our womb, and we will birth His love and vision for others. He will put you in His secret place to know such love you cannot understand or comprehend it. This love can heal the past and bring pleasure and joy to the future. We can open up our hearts before the Lord and trust Him for our past and for what He has for us in our new beginnings with Him. I encourage you to seek Him in the chamber that flows with the river of His love that will overtake you. Jesus is waiting, saying, "Come to Me, I am here waiting for you; meet me in this place and you will be filled with a love that passes your knowledge." He desires us to have the fullness of God dwelling in us.

Oh what an awesome and wonderful love!

My Prayer

Oh Lord, I read the wonderful passage that shows your awesome love for me. The passion you have shown by touching me from my feet all the way to the top of my head. You brought me in by touching me in places that had not been touched or seen. Oh Lord, I desire to come into Your chambers for a time of intimacy with you. Beckon me, and I will come. I want to sit at your feet so that you can cover me with your protective arms. I long for you to look into my eyes, Lord, and tell me all over again just how much you love me. Your passion for me brings me to a place of awe, and I cannot help but smile as I think about your love. Help me to recognize and accept my value and purpose as a woman. Fill me with your Holy Spirit so that I can learn to submit to your will. Then, teach me the beauty of submission, so that I do not wrestle against your hand.

What is Your View from Your Window?

1. Write down your new definition of love, after learning from this chapter.

2. Write down how you have experienced love in your life. How are these experiences similar to your new definition of love? How are they different?

3. When do you have time to spend intimate time with the Lord? If you have not established a time with the Lord, express to Him, in writing how you long to spend this special time with Him. Some of us do not know where to get started. Just sit down by the window, tell Him your heart's desire, and allow the Holy Spirit to lead you to this place of intimacy.

CHAPTER SEVEN
The Season of Building Faith

She girded her loins with strength,
and strengthened her arms.
(Proverbs 31:17)

In this season of my life, God led me on an in-depth biographical study of the "Virtuous Woman" in the book of Proverbs. In the past, whenever I read the infamous question that is asked in that chapter, "who can find a virtuous wife?" I could not help but think that no one could find a woman who could do all of those things well!

Defeated by the same Word designed to make me an over comer, I confessed my inadequacies and turned the page. I later read, a few books over in my Bible, that I can do all things through Christ who strengthens me. Yet, for some reason, I never thought that I could be like the virtuous woman. For one thing, I did not know how to balance my life and all of the responsibilities that God had given me. Then one day God helped me to see that the scripture was not just describing a woman from the Old Testament; it was also describing the woman God was shaping me to be.

In Need Of The Leading Of The Holy Spirit

I can remember when I was very disorganized in every area of my life, and I am still asking the Lord to help me grow in this area. I do not know what I would have done if the Holy Spirit had not come into my life and taken me on a journey, changing my life from glory to glory. In February 1993, I begin to read a book called, <u>The Spirit-Controlled Woman</u>, by Beverly LaHaye. In her book,

91

she talks about the temperament and the Spirit-filled life from a woman's point of view. She spoke about a temperament that described me very well. This temperament was called Sarah Sanguine. Listen to some of her weaknesses: lacks self-control, restless, emotionally unpredictable, not attentive, dominates conversations, seeks credit and approval, completely disorganized, undependable, late, undisciplined, wastes time talking when should be working, many unfinished projects, easily distracted, and falls short of her goals.

The personality of Sarah disturbed me during this season of my life. I could see myself in her, and I did not like it at all. I could see my desperate need for the Holy Spirit to change me and help me to come under the control of His leading. I also saw so much junk in my heart that I had no clue was hiding there. The Lord tells us in *Jeremiah 17:9-10, "The heart is deceitful above all things and beyond cure. Who can understand it? I the Lord search the heart and examine the mind...to reward a man according to his conduct, according to what his deeds deserved."*

What does it mean, that the heart is deceitful or wicked? There are things that are bound up in our hearts that we do not understand. There are situations and incidents in our lives that we do not remember, and some we do not want to remember, because it was a very painful time. We can have unforgiveness, lust, discord, jealousy, envy, and the list goes on in our hearts, and we are not aware of it. Many times, people have come to me and have said that they forgave an individual who had hurt them, but their words and actions did not show forgiveness for that person. You could still hear the hurt and anger as they spoke. They thought, if they repented and cleared their conscience, then everything was okay.

Well, they only cleared their conscience, but not their

heart. The Holy Spirit is the only one that can do that kind of surgery on our hearts. We are not equipped to go into our hearts and try to fix or heal ourselves. We must open our heart to God and let HIM FIX ALL THOSE BROKEN AREAS THAT WE DID NOT ASK TO HAPPEN IN OUR LIVES.

Challenge to Face the Truth

An incident started some years ago, when I owned and operated a T-shirt and computer word processing business. My husband and I were very active in the church we were helping to pioneer, and oftentimes services were held in our home. In addition to that, I lead the women's ministry that was steadily growing, and somehow managed to squeeze in a few speaking engagements in my already full schedule. Did I mention that I had five children at the time, and all of this was very demanding and quite challenging?

I managed to keep everything in perspective, even though my plate was full, everything, that is, except my wifely duties. One day, my husband came home from work and asked me if I had washed and ironed his shirts for the week. Instantly I thought, "And just when was I supposed to have time to do that?" After all, he of all people should have understood the intense pressure that I was under during that season of my life. I could not believe how insensitive he was to my overwhelmingly busy schedule. Sure, I had neglected him; nevertheless, it was not my intention, and he should have known that. This time, I knew I was right!

That day, I bowed before the Lord and cried out, "It's not fair. Why are women expected to do so much and be so much all at the same time?" I just knew that God would send me a maid who knew how to balance the cooking, cleaning, washing, and ironing that I was so behind on during that time. Instead, God told me to sit down from my busy schedule and disorganized life so He could teach me how to balance my responsibilities, love my husband, and serve my family and others more effectively. Only a living God can do that!

Through many tears and much tribulation, God began to mold me by His Word. I must be honest; there were times that I did not feel like adhering to God's instructions to me concerning my husband, but I did not have the heart to rebel against God and turn away from His Word. As I began to surrender to God all that I was, I realized that just as my husband depended on me in our marriage, I needed to have that same kind of dependency on God to help me succeed in every area of my life.

When I accepted that God was not interested in hearing about who was right or wrong in that situation, but was concerned with my understanding of one very simple principle—that apart from Him, I could do nothing, I was more able to enjoy the journey to a better me. God wanted me to bring my busy life to Him, so that He could show me how to operate my business, my marriage, and my family out of His strength and not my own.

Strength Through Trusting God

Today, after having faced numerous trials that pruned my branches, I have learned to rejoice in my tribulations, because I know that in each circumstance, my faith and love for God are being strengthened. In order for Him to teach me this great truth, I had to spend time in prayer, study His Word, and depend on Him to strengthen me each day.

God wants us to be planted and secure in who He is. In

Jeremiah 17:7, the prophet declares:

> *"Blessed is the man who trusts in the Lord. And whose hope is the Lord For he shall be like a tree planted by the waters, which spreads out its roots by the rivers, and will not fear when heat comes but its leaf will be green, and will not be anxious in the year of a drought, nor will cease from yielding fruit."*

This is an awesome scripture, viable for any woman desiring to work toward the high calling of becoming a virtuous woman. Our roots will grow deep in Him so we will be able to handle the hard times and the storms that come our way. We will be rooted and grounded in His love, as we trust in Him. In *Proverbs 31*, we can read about the virtuous woman, and how she prospered by trusting in God. By studying her character, we will learn that she strengthened her spiritual muscles by believing God for the promises He had for her. I hope that by applying some basic principles, we will also be able to see God's provision for your every need, without fear, because it pleases God when we trust Him.

Hope That Endures to the End

Before we visit the virtuous woman in depth, I want to share a few other scriptures that were instrumental in my liberation. In *Hebrews 3:6*, it says, *"...but Christ is a Son over His own house, whose house we are if we hold fast the confidence and the rejoicing of the hope firm to the end."* In other words, Christ, our Shepherd and Savior, has ownership over our house/temple, and He is watching out for our well-being. Therefore, we should hold fast to our confidence, or faith in Him, by enduring to the end.

The words "hold fast" mean something used to hold or secure a thing in place. When we hold fast to our belief in Him, we are rooted and grounded in His love for us. If we do not, *Hebrews 3:18* makes it very clear that we will not enter into His rest, *"And to whom did He swear that they would not enter His rest, but to those who did not obey?"* The Lord tells us if we do not believe in Him, it is rebellion to Him, and who He is in your life. That keeps us from entering into His rest and peace for our daily life.

"Many daughters have done well, but you excel them all." I believe that the "Virtuous Woman" excelled because she allowed God to nurture, heal, and teach her His love, not the love of the world. This love caused her to trust Him through this awesome love relationship. This was my prayer for my life, to excel and overcome. We must have an ear to hear the Spirit of the Lord, because that is the only way we can become virtuous and be over comers. *"He who has an ear, let him hear what the Spirit says to the churches. To him who overcomes, I will give to eat from the tree of life, which is in the midst of the Paradise of God."* *(Revelation 2:7)*

We must ask God to help us to be over comers so we can eat from the tree that brings life, not death. It is His desire to give us His abundance of life, which is the restoration of our souls, and brings peace to our entire being.

The Word asked the question, *"Who can find a virtuous wife? For her worth is far above rubies."* We must stop there and ask the question, Lord do I really know my worth in Christ Jesus? Do I see myself as God sees me?

Do we find ourselves giving in to the moments of our sorrow, disappointments, and failures? Do we strive to be like Christ in every way, by waiting patiently as He changes us from glory to glory? He tells us that we can do all things through Christ Jesus who strengthens us. We must believe in His Word, because it is His Word that strengthens us as we study and meditate on it day and night. The Lord is looking for us to be women who are virtuous and know our worth in Him.

The Lord placed the Virtuous Woman in His Word to encourage us, not to discourage us. When we tell ourselves we could never possess such qualities and discipline in our lives or walk in such strength and faith for the promises of God, we allow the enemy to steal the Word from us. The Word of God is true and living, and firmly tells us that we can do all things through Christ who strengthens us. Let us take a closer look at her qualities and ask God to help us in every area of our lives:

- *She is well trusted by her husband.* She was a woman of integrity and character. (v-11)
- *Her husband will never lack and he will always gain because of her virtue.* She put herself in a position to bless her husband rather than take from him. (v-12)
- *She is good to him at all times.* She pushed aside her own tiredness and needs to minister to her husband. (v-11)
- *She shops wisely.* She was not an impulsive buyer, but one who counts the cost. (vs-14, 16)
- *She is very strong.* She was confident in her ability to handle difficult situations. (v-17)
- *She took care of herself.* She recognized her value and set aside time for herself. (v-22)
- *She willingly works with her hands.* She was an innovative and creative businessperson. (vs-13, 24)
- *She cooks for the entire household and others.* She

nurtured the needs of those even beyond her own home. (v-15)

- *Everything she touched was blessed.* She maintained a daily relationship with the Lord through consistent times of prayer. (v- 16) She planned and prepared for the next season. She considered the cares of tomorrow without taking on its worries by planning and organizing. (v- 21)
- *She spoke with wisdom.* She spent time in prayer, allowing the Holy Spirit to teach her the ways of the Lord. (v-26)
- *She took care of her home.* She set the atmosphere of her home with prayer and much love. (v-27)
- *She knew how to manage her time and did not waste it.* She learned how to discipline her time. (v-27)
- *She took care of her children.* She accepted her role and the responsibilities of being a mother. (v-28)
- *Wherever she sowed, she reaped a good harvest.* She knew the importance of giving. (v-18)
- *She makes herself available.* She was hospitable. (v-15)
- *She takes care of the needy.* She believed in outreach ministry and met the needs of others. (v-20)
- *She is confident and courageous.* She allowed the testing and trials of life to mature her faith in God. (v-25)

When I read about the virtuous woman, I wondered how long it took her to become this great example to all women. Who taught her how to be this woman of excellence? I am convinced that it was God himself who taught her, and He desires to teach us, too. Perhaps you have read about her and thought you could never live up to her reputation; nevertheless, you can. The one assurance I have of that is this: The Word of God did not say she was perfect; it said she was virtuous. To have virtue means to be of moral excellence and goodness. This character is the very nature of God. Moreover, since it is His perfect will that we would be conformed to

His image, He will not disappoint us in our endeavor, because He desires for all of us to be overcomers in our daily walk with Him.

I can look at those qualities that were listed about her, and see that I have grown over the years. Now I am able to say, "Thank you, Lord, for helping me learn how to manage my time and rest in You." In other areas, I can say Lord, I need your help. I am sure that the virtuous woman cried out the same way and asked the Holy Spirit help her. You can see as you read about her accomplishments that she had a loving relationship with the Lord on a continuous basis. That relationship helped her to develop these valuable characteristics and fruit she was bearing. She spent time learning how to pray and receiving wisdom from other women who had already walked this out with the Lord. She drew from the well of prayer and wisdom.

My Prayer

Dear Lord, thank you, for giving me an example in your Word of a Godly woman, with so many tasks and responsibilities. Each time I consider her, I am encouraged to strive for excellence instead of fearing my shortcomings in comparison to her greatness. Like her, there are so many wise women for me to glean from in this season of my life. Teach me how to sit among wise women who will teach me your ways. I know that the process will take time, but my heart is open to you, and I am willing to learn. God, I know I can do it, because you told me yourself that I could do all things through Christ who strengthens me.

Lord, help me in the areas that I must be a woman of faith, who will trust you to organize my spiritual life as well as my daily life with my family. I need you to continue to strengthen my spiritual muscles of faith. I want to be led by the Holy Spirit, so He can mold my temperament, and I can understand who I am in You. I know this is a process and it will take time, but my heart is open.

What is Your View from Your Window?

1. Do you find yourself wondering if you are going to ever be able to get it together in areas that you have been asking God to work on? Write down those areas in which you are lacking His perfection and ask Him again to work in love in these areas of your life.

2. Why is it so hard to believe that God can fix those areas of our lives and move us into our promised land?

3. What is the one trial that you have gone through in which you were able to see the hands of God? How has this trial helped you to see Jesus working in your life, or do you have a hard time seeing God in this situation? Express your concern to God and wait patiently for a loving answer. Take a moment to look through your window and find out what He wants to say to you today!!!

CHAPTER EIGHT
The Season of the Sabbath

*Take delight in the Lord and He will give you
the desires of your heart.
(Psalms 37:4)*

*The Sabbath Day is just for you,
To cease from all the work you do,
A time for you to lie down and rest,
To rise renewed at your very best.*

This section of the book is to lay some solid foundation on what God expects from us, as His children, when it comes to rest. Just imagine, He set a day aside just so we can rest, and be revived from the intense hard work of the week. We use the word "Sabbath" because that is what God called it, which simply means rest.

It is important for us to not only acknowledge the Sabbath but to partake of it as well. God set the Sabbath day apart and became our example as to how we should honor that time. We must know that God established a time of rest for us—not just for Himself. He is a God who lives and sets examples for His children. According to *Genesis 2:2*, God had finished all of His creation on the sixth day, and rested on the seventh day.

We know that when God rested, it was very different from the way that we are to rest. For us, we can look at the word "rest" and apply it to our Sabbath. Rest means a period of not using any energy, but just being quiet and at ease, especially after working or being active. This means freedom from worry, trouble, or pain, and enjoying quietness and peace of mind. Rest is also the condition of being still, not moving; to stop work or other activity in order to refresh oneself. Webster's definition continues:

to give rest, to support or be supported, to lay or lie (Rest your head on the pillow).

Today, we are so inundated with duties and responsibilities; meeting expectations; and setting goals; that resting seems more like a pastime than a reality. To many believers, laws established in the Old Testament do not apply today, including the law concerning the Sabbath. They have somehow disregarded the Old Testament and only consider the New Testament to be God's law for today. However, this was not Jesus' view of the Old Testament law. In *Matthew 5:17*, Jesus said, *"Do not think that I came to destroy the Law or the Prophets. I did not come to destroy but to fulfill."* Jesus came to fulfill the commandments of God through a loving relationship, not condemnation.

It is a Commandment

We must ask ourselves why we should have a Sabbath a day of rest. **It is a commandment.** *"Remember the Sabbath day, to keep it holy."* (Exodus 20:8) He did not change that commandment. It amazes me how we can teach in Sunday classes and teach our children that it is a sin to steal, kill, and commit adultery, while we totally disregard this time of rest that Gods requires from us in our relationship with Him. We can see how important it is to obey nine of the commandments, because they look like obvious sin to us. Why is it so hard to see that when we refuse to rest as God commanded us to do that it is also sin in our lives? **We fight the very commandment that comes to bless us.**

The scriptures tell us in *I Chronicles 28:8-9*, *"Be careful to seek out all the commandments of the Lord your God, that you may possess this good land and leave it as an inheritance for your children after you forever."* God is not saying that when we do nine of His commandments, we possess the goodness of the land and leave an inheritance for our children. We need to stop living our lives for ourselves and think about the inheritance we leave with our children. They can inherit the rest that God has led us into for our life. This is an eternal principle that all of us should see; that God wanted our bodies to be refreshed and well-rested.

We Are Blessed in Keeping the Sabbath

"If you turn away your foot from the Sabbath, from doing your pleasure on My holy day, and call the Sabbath a delight, the holy day of the Lord honorable, and shall honor Him, not doing your own ways nor finding your own pleasure, not speaking your own words, then you shall delight yourself in the Lord; and I will cause you to ride on the high hills of the earth, and feed you with the heritage of Jacob your father. The mouth of the Lord has spoken." *(Isaiah 58:13-14)*

This Word blessed me so much as God began to teach me about resting in Him. When we want to please God, He in return wants to bless us. He spoke to me in a gentle way as He said, "If you delight in my day of rest by honoring Me, then I will give you the desires of your heart. The Lord is asking us to set a day aside that will honor Him, a time that you can ask the Father what He wants to do on your day of rest, to tell Him that you have set it aside as a holy day before Him. He wants to hear your voice say, *"Lord, this is your day; let me delight in it with a heart of love and passion for you."*

I was reminded of the *Psalm 37:3*, which says if you delight in the Lord, He give will you the desires of your heart. The word "delight" means a high degree of pleasure or enjoyment. We just read in *Isaiah 58:13-14* the Lord called the Sabbath a great pleasure and enjoyment, and when we have this same pleasure for Him, He will give us the desires of our hearts. When we take the time to set a day aside for a Sabbath and ask the Lord what is it that He wants to do on this day, I believe He looks into our eyes and asks us what we want to do. Because my desires become His desires, whatever pleases us in our day of rest pleases Him, since we have honored Him in this day.

When we have a personal relationship with God, our time with Him is personal. I cannot put you in bondage to a law that you do not understand or keep. The Lord is the only one who can take you into that place of understanding and help you through your relationship with Him. A day of rest for me is a delight, because the Lord gives me the desires of my heart out of our time spent together. You, too, will see the blessing of the Lord as you begin to learn to walk in a biblical principle that will bring you freedom.

Jesus is the Lord of the Sabbath. Therefore, our submission is to Jesus. Because He is the Lord of the Sabbath, and we were made for the Lord, we do what God wants us to do with that day. Jesus came to establish a loving relationship with us as we spend time with Him and we hear His heart. Remember, He did not come to change the law, but to fulfill it according to the will of the Father.

We must stop and hear from the Holy Spirit about the day we set aside as our day of rest. This day is set apart to be holy. What is it He wants us to do? If He says it's okay to sleep, then sleep; if He allows you to read, then read;

garden, then garden. Our relationship with God is personal; that is why we must hear from God ourselves. Then we can please Him, not a man, but God. This is an awesome scripture to me, because God is asking us to do something that will bring blessing to our soul.

> *"Bless the Lord, O my soul; and all that is within me, bless His holy name! Bless the Lord, O my soul and forget not all His benefits; Who forgives all your iniquities, who heals all your diseases, who redeems your life from destruction, who crowns you with loving kindness and tender mercies, who satisfies your mouth with good things, so that your youth is renewed like the eagle's. (Psalms 103:1-3)*

When we bless Him with our soul, we are saying with our mind, will, and emotions, "Lord, I am blessing you." When we bless the Lord, He in return blesses us with all His benefits and much more. He wants to renew our strength so we can be able to handle our season and to help us through each window of our lives.

God Established It As Holy

In the beginning, when God created the first six days, He looked at what He had made and said it was good. When He established the seventh day, He ceased from His labor, blessed the seventh day, and made it holy. *"Then God blessed the seventh day and sanctified it ...". (Genesis 2)* God set an example for us because he knew we would need a day to be replenished and refreshed, so we could make it through the rest of the week. When He said He sanctified it, God made it a day set apart for His glory, a day to honor Him. He is the only one who can help us make it through each moment, day, week, month or year. **We must honor Him for His faithfulness and His love for us as His children.**

We live in such a busy and fast-paced life that we do not even realize how much we miss because we are too busy to stop and smell the roses. Our children have grown up and left home, and we do not even remember their transition into young adulthood. Our spouses are sporting new makeovers, and we have not even noticed the change. We have become so busy in life that the little things, like rest, are insignificant to us and often taken for granted.

Like any other commandment in the Word of God, we have the option to obey and receive God's blessings, or disobey and experience the consequences that are sure to follow *(Deuteronomy 30:11-20)*. Since God delights in our willingness to obey Him more than our sacrifice of hard work *(1 Samuel 15:22)*, He won't force us to take a day of rest. He will, however, allow situations and circumstances in our lives that will make resting an essential part to our recovery or healing process.

God does not look at our works, but our heart. He is looking for a heart that is yielded to Him and His Word. When we are exhausted and burned out from work and lack of rest, we are more useful to the devil than we are to God. The devil knows that if we stay too busy, we will not be as effective in our prayers, studying God's word, or even ministering to others. In our tired and burned out condition, we can expect to lose some of our greatest battles both physically and spiritually.

Physically, we are more susceptible to sickness and disease. We lack patience with others and are easily angered. Spiritually, we are unable to spend quiet, intimate time alone with God. Thus, our ability to hear Him is lessened, and in our hurriedness, we miss the warnings that God uses as signals to keep us from going the wrong way.

> *"Come to Me, all you who labor and are heavy laden, and I will give you rest. Take My yoke upon you and learn from Me, for I am gentle and lowly in heart, and you will find rest for your souls. For My yoke is easy and My burden is light."* (Matthew 11:28)

Jesus is the Sabbath who came for us that we may find rest and refuge in Him. Whatever we have need of can be found in Him. We have the liberty, as children of God, to come to Him and rest in knowing that He will replenish us and restore our strength.

Practical Wisdom for Your Sabbath

The Sabbath is for our benefit. The Sabbath is designed for our benefit so that God can replenish and rejuvenate us both physically and spiritually. *"And He said to them, 'The Sabbath was made for man, and not man for the Sabbath. Therefore the Son of Man is also Lord of the Sabbath."* (Mark 2:27–28) The Lord shows us in the New Testament that He did not come to remove the Sabbath, but to bring relationship. The Pharisees saw it as a law, a legalistic day that Jesus and His disciples were not honoring. The Lord came to bring relationship and love to our lives, but the religious leaders did not understand His purpose. Their mind was in bondage to the old covenant, but Jesus brought in the new covenant, which brought a love relationship with the Father and His children. By the shedding of blood, there was remission for our sins; in other words, forgiveness.

Hebrew 10:16-18 says, *"This is the covenant that I will make with them after those days, says the Lord; I will put My laws into their hearts and in their minds I will write them."* Now Christ lives in us and His word lives in our hearts. The Lord had to remind them that this day was not for religious acts that cause us to feel bound. The Sabbath was for us to be liberated to worship and please God through relationship. We must remember Jesus is the Lord of our day of rest and every moment of our lives.

Sleep During Your Sabbath

You should not feel that in order for your Sabbath to be holy, you must read the Word of God and pray the entire length of your Sabbath. It is okay to lie down and go to sleep! In fact, sleeping during your Sabbath is spiritual, because God wants you to be refreshed (refreshed means to provide vigor, healthy physical and mental energy or power). God wants you to rest so that you can have the energy you need to be effectively used by Him. Be careful not to put yourself in bondage by treating your time of rest like a rule or law. Relax, and let the Lord fill you up. You cannot pray, understand the Word of God, or hear from God when you are fatigued. God is not as complicated as we have made Him to be. He understands our bodies better than we do, and He knows exactly what we need.

Share Your Sabbath

We cannot be selfish on our day of rest. I had to understand that once my husband and children came home, I had to make sure I served them. Jesus wants to make sure that we do not make the Sabbath a selfish religious day. We must remember that we are still here for each other. We see in Mark 3:1-5 that Jesus went into the synagogue and saw a man with a deformed hand.

He questioned the Pharisees about their attitude toward doing a good deed on the Sabbath. He was angry at their hardened hearts, and He healed the man.

In *I Samuel 21:1-6* David fed his men bread from the Tabernacle. This bread, called the Bread of the Presence, symbolized God's presence among His people as well as His loving care that met physical needs. David had relationship with God, and the Lord knew the intent of David's heart. Jesus demonstrated that the Sabbath is a day to do good deeds. God provided the Sabbath as a day of rest and worship. He did not intend for us to become so involved with rest that we fail to help others in need. You have to use wisdom to discern a genuine need. Both Jesus and David understood that the intent of God's law was to promote love for God and others.

Seek the True Meaning of Sabbath

The Sabbath day is a day set apart for God to restore you and bring love, peace, and joy to your life. I have seen people who misunderstood the Sabbath by saying, "I have to leave the ministry," when it becomes overwhelming, or "I cannot deal with people right now," because God is dealing with them. There may be a time when we need to get away, but sometimes we do it with the wrong attitude and motivation of heart. We do not even realize it, but oftentimes we hurt others by ignoring them or pushing them aside. God wants us to show love toward one another. We must be sensitive to others when we pull away to rest. If not, we'll soon find that we are not engaging in a true Sabbath, which God has sanctified for

Himself, but just simply pulling away. He does not want us to offend others. When we do, we must stop, repent, and reconcile with our brother.

> *"Therefore if you bring your gift to the altar, and there remember that your brother has something against you, leave your gift there before the altar, and go your way, first be reconciled to your brother, and then come and offer your gift." (Matthew 5:23)*

The Lord wants us to be able to come to Him with a pure heart, dealing with unforgiveness and hurt. Let Him deal with those areas that will keep us from our time of rest with Him. If you set order in your life, clean your windows, and make the time to rest, then God can fill your cup. When you are walking in His presence, you are able to walk in love with others.

The list below is broken down for you to use as a tool for a reminder on how to establish your day of rest. Place it in your journal so you can keep it before you at all times. Please, also take this list and share it with others who do not understand how to start a day of rest.

Establishing a Day of Rest

- **Ask the Lord for a rest day; your personal day of rest.** Ask Him to help you set aside that time. Start slowly, and work yourself up to a full day if you cannot fit an entire day in your weekly schedule immediately. You can start with a half of day if you work all week, and Saturday is filled with responsibilities for the family. You must start somewhere, because you need this rest.

- **It is very important that you communicate what you are doing** and how you would like to have a day set aside for resting. Go to your family, roommate, and others who live with you, and in love, share with them what you would like to do. Please pray first and ask the **Holy Spirit to touch their hearts.** If you are living with an unsaved spouse who does not understand the ways of God, he or she could be resistant to your plan. Pray for your spouse and give God time to work on their hearts. **Continue to serve them and love them through this season, until God opens up the door of Heaven for you.** It will come.

- **Do not make this a religious day with rules, feeling that you cannot rest.** Going to sleep is spiritual, because God said He wanted you to be refreshed. **Refreshed means to provide vigor (healthy physical and mental energy, or power).** He wants you to rest for your health, so that you will have energy to be used by Him effectively. **Delight in Him, and He will give you the desires of your heart. Ask the Lord of your rest day what He wants to do. He is faithful to respond in love!**

- **We cannot be selfish on our day of rest.** I had to understand that once my husband and children came home on my day of rest, I had to cook and make sure I served them. Jesus wants to make sure we don't make the Sabbath a selfish, religious day.

- **Discipline yourself so that it becomes a lifestyle and second nature.** Remember that this is a process. **It will take time!** Make the effort and start working in your planner and journal. Begin to look at your week and plan your entire day, week and month out first. Your goal is to take one day at a time. Schedule each window with your responsibilities for that day. Look at your sample sheet and use it as a pattern. Look at your priorities for each day.

My Prayer

Dear Lord, help me to understand that the Sabbath was made for me. I recognize that it is a holy day that you set apart for me to rest and be restored. I desire to establish and maintain a genuine relationship with you in my time of resting and do not want to make the Sabbath some religious ritual. Help me to plan my Sabbath so that I may enter into your rest.

I need the Sabbath in order to serve in my family, in the ministry, and in the kingdom of God. I know my schedule and responsibilities are hectic, but you know my heart. Continue to teach me how to delight in Your Sabbath. I so desire to trust You and what You have for me. I want to please You in every way, and I will bless You, Lord, with my soul and all that is within me, and I will bless your holy name.

What is Your View from Your Window?

1. Write three things that would hinder you from establishing your day of rest. What will you do about them?

2. Write three steps you will take to establish your day of rest.

3. At this point, if you have any frustration, stop and pray. Ask God to help you establish your day of rest. Tell Him your frustration and pray about it.

CHAPTER NINE
The Season of Testing

*"For I know the thoughts that I think towards you,
says the Lord, thoughts of peace and not of evil,
to give you a future and a hope".
(Jeremiah 29:11)*

A dear friend of mine shared with me a popular cartoon that airs on Saturday mornings, and it happened to be a great example for this chapter. There was a whiz kid who won the Science Fair every year without trouble. It was time for the Science Fair again at the school where she attended, and she was definitely a favorite to win again. In the cartoon, a younger girl, who admired the whiz kid and her work for science, befriended her. Unsuspectingly, the whiz kid let her new friend in on her science secrets, and she let her help to complete the project that she planned to enter for the Science Fair. Her prodigy watched intently, took notes until she knew what materials were needed, and what formulas were required to duplicate the project.

When the whiz kid realized that she had forgotten to turn in her entry form, her new friend kindly offered to drop it by the school on her way home. The next day, when the whiz kid brought in her project, she learned that her entry form had not been received, and therefore, she could not participate. But that disappointment was only met by utter disgust when she watched the Science Fair, and found that her new friend had not only won, but won it with her creation!

When the judges asked the little girl to explain how her creation worked, she stumbled in her words. She had befriended the whiz kid long enough to learn how to duplicate the project but never inquired about what made it work. When the whiz kid saw the sweat rolling down her face, she unselfishly stepped in and offered the answer to the question that had mystified the little girl. The judges walked away highly impressed with the little girl.

When we lack people skills and are not sensitive to others, we tend to walk right over them to accomplish the task that has been given to us. We somehow manage to blame our test of tolerance on others' incompetence, and neglect to see that God is actually administering a test of character. It is not until God has tallied up our scores that we learn that we have failed the portions of the test on love, patience, and gentleness.

I was the type of person who just had to have everything under control. I was not a fanatic, but I did need to make sure things were organized and precise so that I could move forward with my plan of action. I mentioned earlier about my temperament being a sanguine, which means fun loving, and living for today—not tomorrow. As I continued to grow through the control and leading of the Holy Spirit, I was continuing to learn more about myself. One of the things I learned was that my dominating temperament in this season of my life was Clara Choleric. Sara Sanguine was not my dominating temperament; she was only dominating in that season of my life because of my past hurts, which caused me to desire to be the life of the party.

Now that the Holy Spirit had taken me through a process of healing, she had taken a back seat to Clara Choleric. Beverly LaHaye describes her as one that, "loves activity. Clara is extremely goal-oriented, which may account for her boundless energy. Her busy mind can always find something for her do, and most of it is meaningful. Clara is extremely outspoken, opinionated, strong-willed, and fearless. This is a problem for cholerics that the other two more introverted temperaments do not have, and it becomes apparent whenever they are not controlled by the Holy Spirit. Their mouth usually gives them away. It also adds to their natural anger problem, which causes them to overtly express themselves.

I admire Clara's organizational skills, her gifts, and ability to keep order in her life, but unfortunately, if her character has not been pruned to produce the fruit of the Holy Spirit, Clara may think more highly of herself than she ought to think, and less of others who are not just like her. In other words, Clara will become prideful and arrogant in her gifts. Regardless of what temperament dominates, it must be under the control of the Holy Spirit.

God made each of us different so that anyone who is in Christ Jesus could bring his or her uniqueness to the Kingdom of God. Whether we like to admit it or not, we need one another to be all that God intends for us to be. That is how God designed it to be, and we might as well accept it! I learned this lesson the hard way.

Testing My Character

Several years ago, when my husband and I were working in a children's ministry at a large church, we were preparing to have a practice fire drill for the children. This drill was designed to prepare the volunteer staff workers in case of a disaster, and to test their ability to safeguard the children, without leaving any of them behind, or losing them in the crowd of people.

My husband had given all the instructions to the leaders with a strong caution not to let the children out of their sight. Even though we were only evacuating the children, the drill was designed so that a selected crew of workers (we will call them "strangers") from the church would see if they could get the children to go with them away from the designated safe place.

When the drill began, everything was going well, considering we were attempting to usher 900 children out of the building in an orderly fashion. Then it happened. As we were going down the stairs, I saw one of the leaders in the Children's Ministry hand over one of our children to an appointed "stranger." At first, I could not believe my eyes. After all, he knew the purpose of the drill; the individuals who were a part of the Children's Ministry had just received specific instructions not to do that.

Well, when I saw this, I lost it! I mean I really lost it! I headed straight for him with my pointy finger stretched out towards his nose, and started screaming at that leader like I was the wicked witch of the west (as he later described me). Without hesitation, I began to tell this volunteer staff leader that he was irresponsible, and questioned his ability to understand simple instructions, such as the ones he had just received. Oh, it was not a pretty sight, especially to those who were standing around listening to my every cutting word.

Before I could make it up the stairs when the drill was over, the Holy Spirit convicted me for my actions. He allowed me to see that the nature of my sin was pride, and my temperament was out of control. *"Let nothing be done through selfish ambitions or conceit, but in lowliness of mind, let each esteem others better than himself. Let each of you look out not only for his own interests but also for the interests of others."* (Philippians 2:3) That particular day of the fire drill, my character did not resemble God in any way, because I was only concerned about me. Let us examine my character that day more closely.

What was the motivation of my heart? I wanted everyone to see that we had everything under control, but in my attempt to prove that our ministry had everything together, I was actually tearing us apart. My temper was out of control, and I needed to abide in Christ to bear the fruit of gentleness, patience, and self-control. My actions did not just stunt my growth in God, but it possibly impaired others in their growing relationship with God. Sometimes we are driven by our goals and accomplishments, rather than by our hearts.

The Flesh Profits Us Nothing

We have to be careful when we think more highly of ourselves than we should. When we work with others, we should work together as a family or team. It is true that everyone should share the same vision, purpose, or goal. It is also true that everyone should be able to work together in love and peace. Ask yourself, am I lifting myself up, or am I lifting Jesus up through my gifts? You might have peace about your accomplishments, and the way you accomplished them. If so, ask yourself if the people you work or live with have peace when you work with them. Is it possible that they are nervous wrecks, because they could not meet your expectations or be as organized as you are?

When we lack love, joy, long-suffering, gentleness, goodness, faithfulness, self-control, kindness and peace, we are not led by the Holy Spirit. We are led by our flesh, which will profit us nothing. In other words, we cannot accomplish anything of everlasting value if we do not walk in the fruit of the Holy Spirit as described in *Galatians 5:22*. When we walk in pride, contentions, jealousies, anger, selfish ambitions, and dissensions, we cannot experience or inherit the abundance of life that God promised us in His Word.

Was I not justified in how I felt? If the leader had done

the right thing, I would not have lost it. With God, those trivial things do not even matter. He has given me His Word to follow in every circumstance, no matter what. One of the greatest victories we can ever face is when we remove excuses from our lips, and bring forth repentance from our hearts. I had to repent to that leader in front of all the other leaders and share what happened. Even though we were able to laugh about it later, I thank God that this leader forgave me and did not take it to heart. I recognized that I could have caused him to stumble if he were not mature in the Lord. *"We know that we have passed from death to life, because we love the brethren. He who does not love his brother abides in death." (I John 3:14-18)*

Love Your Brother and Sister

When we do not love one another, we do not abide in the light of Jesus. The power of God's love is necessary in our lives. Without the power of love, our windows become darkened, dirty, scratched, or broken. When people look at us, they will not be able to see that God has deposited His precious Holy Spirit inside if us; instead, they will see that our hearts are cold and hardened. In *I John 3:16-17*, it says the following:

> *"By this we know love, because He laid down His life for us. And we also ought to lay down our live for the brethren. But whoever has this world's goods and sees his brother in need, and shuts up his heart from him, how does the love of God abide in him? My little children let us not love in word or in tongue, but in deed and in truth."*

How do we know love? Through Jesus Christ our Savior, who loves us and died for us while we were still lost and dead to our sins. We should aim to be like Jesus in every way and trust that He will teach us how to lay our lives down for our brothers and sisters in the Lord without criticizing or complaining about them because they made a mistake. Instead, we should desire to show them the same love and mercy that God demonstrates to us when we blow it. If our expressed words of love are not validated by our actions, then we are not demonstrating genuine love. We must show love not only by what we say, but by how we treat one another.

My Prayer

Oh Lord, teach me how to walk in love with others. Strip me of my complaining and critical attitude, so that I will not become a stumbling block to anyone. My desire is to demonstrate the fruits of love, patience, and gentleness in every area of my life. I want to be able to help others organize their lives just as you have shown me how to organize mine. I realize that if my heart remains hardened and my windows darkened, no one will be able to see You in me. Cleanse me, Lord, with the light of Your Word, and allow the radiance of Your Spirit to shine through me.

What is Your View from Your Window?

Ask the Holy Spirit to help you if you have a critical tongue or your thoughts are not pure toward other people. Read James 3:5-15 and Psalms 19:12-14 and allow the Holy Spirit to minister to you. Write a page on what He is speaking in your heart.

CHAPTER TEN
The Season of Prayer

"He restores my soul;
he leads me in paths of righteousness for
His namesake."
(Psalms 23:3)

We have already established that prayer is an essential key to total victory in our Christian walk. In order to experience discipline in every area of your life, you must first start with disciplining yourself in daily prayer. Start slowly and work your way there.

Second, take the time to establish a prayer journal as you talk to God about your ups and downs. Use your journal to record answered prayers, God's instructions, and the gentle words He whispers to your heart. A journal is a wonderful way of capturing those precious moments spent in the presence of the Lord. If we do not record them, we tend to move on to the next crisis without even acknowledging that God answered our prayers.

I had to discipline myself to release myself to the Lord and share my heart with Him. As I wrote my intimate thoughts in my journal, God would speak to me. Then, He would lead me to scriptures that encouraged and built me up for that day or for a specific situation. I could go back and read about the prayers He had answered, that I had forgotten I had prayed during the hard times. Sometimes, we forget what we have prayed, and whether God answered them yet or not.

The reason we forget is that we move on to the next crisis and go on with life. That is not what God wants. Journaling made it easy for me to record my answered prayers, and whenever I needed a personal reminder of God's faithfulness, I read my journal, which was filled with one miracle after another! I can honestly say that journaling played a significant part in my triumphs over the difficult times in my life, because I could see that God cared about me and had been with me every step of the way.

This is necessary in your windows. Scheduling at least 15 minutes to write in your journal is a must. There are no rules about what to write in your journal. It is your personal conversation book with God. Take the liberty to write about such things as your pain, joys, frustrations, faults, dreams, hopes, and even your love for Him. Then, stop and meditate for a minute, and let Him write back to you. He will speak to your heart in ways that you cannot imagine. He delights in talking to us, but we never sit still long enough to let Him speak. So many people say, "I cannot hear God," however, they do not take the time to ask the Holy Spirit to lead them to God's throne so that they can hear His voice.

Make sure that you have your Bible close by when journaling. Many times I have been led in my heart to pick up His word, and without fail, God is faithful to speak through His Word. I can remember when the Lord gave me *Psalms 23* to meditate on during a difficult time in my life. He made it clear that He wanted me to know who He was in my life, and how He planned to care for me. I thought it would be great to end this book with God's reassuring Words. He is our Shepherd and He will provide everything we need. He will make me to lie down and get the rest I need. I do not have sense enough to rest on my own, so He gently makes me lie in a place of rest. He will lead me into a peaceful place in His presence and begin to heal my soul and restore unto me everything the enemy has stolen throughout my life. He leads me to His wisdom and shows me how to walk according to His Word for His glory.

Even though I will go through some difficult days in life, I will not let the enemy put me in fear, because His perfect love casts out all fear. I will rest in His love, because I know He is with me through every step. He will keep and protect me and give me words of encouragement. He will keep my mind at peace. He sets me up high and gives me a feast of His love, joy, and peace in front of the enemy. The Lord will exalt me by anointing my life with His presence. As He fills me up in His presence, He gives me more than enough. I can give my overflow to those who not yet have known Him in this way. Thank God, His mercy and grace are always with me through my daily walk with Him. I will always dwell with my Father in an intimate, loving way, for eternity. It was in times like this that the Lord would take a scripture and talk to me personally in my journal.

As I meditated on that passage of scripture, I was renewed in my spirit and heart. Let us take a closer look at that scripture together. Sometimes, when we read a familiar scripture, we tend to skip right over revelation and just read the words. God's Word is the very breath of God Himself. His Word is alive! Read this wonderful Psalm for yourself and let the Holy Spirit minister to you. But before you read it, I want you to take a minute and pray. Ask the Holy Spirit to impart revelation to you so that you can know God's promise to you.

Psalm 23

"The Lord is my Shepherd, I shall not want..."
The Lord is your Shepherd and Lord of your life. You will not have want for anything, because He will provide everything you need.

"He makes me to lie down in green pastures, He leads me

beside the still waters, He restores my soul..."

He will make you to lie down and give you rest for your soul. Sometimes we do not know we need to be still and lie down in His presence, because we are distracted by so many things. He will lead you into the peaceful place of His presence, where He can heal your soul. The restoration is a renewing of the mind, submitting your will and desires to Him, and your emotions are stabilized by His peace. It is His desire to restore everything the enemy has stolen from you.

"He leads me in the path of righteousness For His Name's sake..."

He will lead you by His wisdom, and show you how to walk according to His Word so that you can glorify Him.

"Yea, though I walk through the Valley of the shadow of death, I will fear no evil For You are with me..."

Even though you will go through some difficult days, do not be afraid because the perfect love that God has for you will cast out all fear. Rest in His love, knowing that He is with you each step of the way. Remember that your valley experiences are only a shadow. You will survive through that season, as He walks with you each step of the way.

"Your rod and Your staff, they comfort me..."

He will comfort and strengthen you with words of encouragement that will surround your mind with absolute peace.

"You prepare a table before me in the presence of my enemies..."

In your honor, He will lift you on high and prepare a feast of His love, joy, and peace before your enemies.

Come to His table of love that is full with His Word, which will feed and nourish you, providing the strength you need to bear these fruit. Learn to abide in Jesus and His Word.

"You anoint my head with oil, My cups runs over..."
Your head will be anointed by the Almighty as you stand in the Presence of the King. All the while, He is pouring His Spirit inside your heart until it overflows with greatness. Now you are filled with His oil that lights you as a lamp, and burns and shines before all men. When our cup runs over, we are able to give out of what He has given us. We must run to that secret place to be filled with His love that overflows into others.

"Surely Your goodness and mercy shall follow me all the days of my life..."
You can be assured that you will never walk alone, for God has sent His goodness and mercy to pursue after you every day for the rest of your life. Think about it, goodness is on one side, and mercy is on the other. They will keep you in those difficult days.

"And I will dwell in the house of the Lord forever."
When you spend time with Him, you will dwell with your heavenly Father for eternity.

Practical Ways of Preparing and Working in Your Prayer Journal

- **Prayer is the key** and the most powerful place where you must discipline yourself on a daily basis. **Start slowly and work your way there.**
- **Take the time to establish a prayer journal**, so you can talk to God about your difficulties.

Journals are the most wonderful **ways of releasing, seeing answered prayer, and wonderful times with the Lord.** This is another place I have found that has kept me through good and bad days. He would gently speak to me as I wrote my intimate thoughts in words.

- **He will lead you to scriptures that encourage and build you up for that day.** You will be able to go back and read where He has answered prayers that you had forgotten you prayed during the hard times. Sometimes we forget what we have prayed and whether God has answered them yet. **The reason we forget is that we move onto the next crisis and go on with life.** That is not what God wants. He wants us to know that He is living, and He cares about everything in our lives. Release yourself to Him, and share your heart with Him every day. I don't know how I would have made it if I had not had my journal time.

- **You must set at least fifteen minutes to write in your journal.** You can write about things such as your pain, joy, frustration, faults, repentance, and your love for Him. **Stop and meditate for a minute, and let Him write back to you. I promise you He wants to commune with you this way.** So many people say, I can't hear God, yet they never **sit still long enough to ask the Holy Spirit to lead** them to God's throne, so that they can hear the still, small voice of God.

- **Make sure you have your Bible close**, because that has been the most effective time of hearing from God that I have received. Many times, I have been led in my heart to pick up His word, and **He speaks through His Word.**

- **We need to see and trust in the promises God**

has set before us in His Word. The Book of Psalms has awesome scriptures to help us pray and meditate. There are so many wonderful promises that God has stored up for us, to help us to trust Him during our seasons.

My Prayer

Thank you, Lord, that You are so personal. I want to learn how to keep a journal so I can express my love and heart to you. I desire an intimate relationship with You that I can carry with me all day. Teach me how to be honest as I write down my intimate thoughts. Through this season of my life, make me lie down in your goodness to restore my soul, which is my mind, will, and emotions. I know the enemy has stolen from me through the sins and hurts of my past. I know that through this surgery of my heart, you will cause me to know your love for my life, and I will dwell in the house of the Lord forever.

What is Your View from Your Window?

1. Take some time to just talk to the Lord. Ask Him what direction He wants for your life. Have a pencil and paper ready to write down what He speaks to your heart.

My Personal Journal

I would like to share a few entries of the answered prayers from my personal journal for a decade of my life. Unfortunately, I did not write down everything God spoke to my husband and me. I am just as confident that He will bring them to pass, nonetheless. As I leafed through my journals and read my entries, I grew all the more encouraged to share them with you.

My best friend, who was there for me the day I started to doubt God, encouraged me greatly. I was scared to death of where He was taking my husband and me. The Lord spoke to Duncan and me years ago about establishing His Church and sharing the gospel with people of many nations. He also spoke to us about this ministry, "*This is Your Season*," that has been established by His hands. We did not know the details of this ministry. We only knew He was going to raise up an international women's ministry one day, which is now being birthed, as you read this book.

When God speaks, we do not know the how, the when, the why, the where, or even the what. We do not know everything that God has planned for us, and that is confirmed by God's Word in *I Corinthians 13:9, "For we know in part and we prophesy in part..."*. But by faith we move with God as He opens up the doors for us. We have had to trust God for each season of our lives, even though we did not always understand them.

Let us look at *Acts 1:7, "And it is not for you to know times or seasons which the Father has put in His own authority."* In this scripture, the disciples were questioning Jesus and wanted to know what was going to happen next. We all want to know what is in store for us. We just have to believe that God has a perfect plan, and He will reveal it to us in His time. I am convinced that if we had not obeyed God and walked by faith when God said to move, we would have missed our season and not been in place for God to take us to the next level.

While God was changing and molding my husband and me, He spoke to us on a continual basis, to encourage us and give us instructions. God used my best friend to keep my arms up while I battled the fear of what people were going to say about my husband and me establishing a church. Through her wisdom from her Bible study on Joshua and Moses, He gave me great victory. She quoted the scriptures about Moses speaking the Word to Joshua on a continuous basis. Joshua heard the promises of God from Moses all the time while He was speaking to the people and to Joshua. God has done the same for us. Month after month, year after year, God has spoken words of encouragement about His plans for our lives.

The entries that you are about to read are not the expressed words of man, but the very voice of God, as He spoke to me during those intimate times I spent seeking His face. These words of encouragement and instruction are priceless and dear to me, but I believe God wants me to share them with you, so that you can know that He desires to speak to you about His plans for your life. It is my prayer that you, too, would experience the love letters from our living God as He pens His response to your prayers.

You must know, this is your season where you will find rest for your soul. Go to Jesus and let Him carry your burdens and bring rest to your mind, will, and emotions. It is my prayer that you will receive the awesome peace that only He can give. As you read the words of Jesus speaking to my soul, I hope you hear the voice of the Lord whispering those words of love into your ear. This is your window of opportunity.

Secret Love Notes From My Personal Journal

1992

You must wait until the Lord releases you for such a ministry. I have so much to teach you, Daughter. You are my servant. I have anointed you to do these things. You will walk as I walked, with much love and authority. You must learn to walk in this way. You are filled with the Holy Spirit, He will teach you. Are you ready?

Yes, Lord, I am ready.

I miss you; I want to walk with you closer. I love you, Dolores.

I love you, Lord.

Wait on Me to go out and preach My words to this dying nation. I will use My son, Duncan, to do mighty works in My Name. I will carry him in My hands. Duncan will hear me, and he will move as I have spoken to him. Be patient. I will do as I said. I love your family!

December 26 1992

Lord, where do I take possession in prayer?

The doors are opened up for you to pray for the sick. You will be used as a chosen vessel for Me to heal others. You must see that you will walk in My light. I will teach you all things. You must listen and read the Word. You will minister to many others.

What are you saying, Lord?

Let Duncan take over in every aspect of your lives. Sit down and go home. You will let this women's ministry go for a SEASON. I will raise it up in its season. You will intercede and let Duncan be raised up. Yes, be silent when he is present with others; listen to him. I will speak to Duncan. I will raise up the people to carry on My work here. Now pray and let go. Let him be raised up for My purpose.

Do not start anything now. I will raise up the women's ministry. I will speak to your heart. This is My desire, Daughter; I will raise it up as I have spoken to you. I love you Dolores, I have come to sup with you. Seek me and you will find me. Yes, you will intercede as I call you to do.

What are you saying to me, Lord?

I will take care of you Dolores. Do not ask Me where you are going, trust Me. Seek Me and fellowship with Me, and do not seek for a place, just wait on Me. You will fast for three days and seek Me. You will not ask Duncan about moving, or talk to anyone else about moving. You will seek Me only and make no plans. Stay with Me for the next 3 days. I love you Dolores.

I love You, Lord.

Duncan is in my hand, nothing will come against him. I have chosen him for My purposes. He will see My hand in the midst of your family. My daughter, Bertha, is surely protected. She has been called back home for My purposes. You must stand strong in faith. I love you and your family. Love your family and trust Me.

I never, Lord, had so much peace and faith. I know I get impatient at times, but I believe you will come through for us. I trust and love you, Lord.

Yes, rejoice My daughter, because I have visited you today. Be still and quiet and let the Lord move. He has visited you this day. He is pleased with you and your family. He desires you as a warrior for Him.

Is this message for Duncan as well?

Yes, My daughter. I will speak these words into both of you. I have chosen him as a priest for My purposes. If you both will keep My ways and walk in them, I will cause you to be shepherds over My house and My people. I will send you to a place for my purposes.

Lord I long for You. I love You. I want to seek your face.

Oh, I love you. Dolores, I love you, Seek My face and you will find Me. I am with you forever.

January 1993
Matthew 28:18

Dolores, know that I have authority over all things. I have given you that authority to go out and take dominion over the darkness of this world. I am strong in you, Daughter. I will demonstrate My power.

Walking in the Spirit is not a mystical exercise in which a person is in some kind of trance, nor is it a feeling. Walking in the Spirit is a constant love of fellowship and communing with the Son of God. It is a part of every activity in your life. Eating, inviting Him to the table, cooking, and serving in your home is a time with Him, not just a time of prayer, but a continual communication to remain in every moment of our lives. It is a continual love for Him. "I do not just love You when I pray, but all day long, moment by moment."

March 1993

Daughter, you must pray in the night. Yes, go and pray in the night, a time of intercession into night. Yes, you can pray during the night. Dolores, I will call on you. You must make yourself available. Seek Me, you shall find me day and night. I am calling you to pray. This is why I have called you to pray for My people.

I love you, Lord. I love praying and lifting people up before you, God. I love to encourage and fellowship with Your people. I have prayed and fasted about my commitment to this ministry of prayer. You, oh Lord, have placed this on my heart to pray, and this is where you want me to be.

I am drawing you now, Dolores. Listen, to the Word of God. Now listen. I am drawing you near to Me.

May 1994
Isaiah 8

Write the vision. You will bring forth My vision. She will grow and you will watch her grow. You will see many visions. Vision after vision, says God. You will see them all come to pass. You will not leave this place until every vision comes to pass, says God. You must be humble and broken in every way, says God. Nothing will come of yourself, not your flesh. It will only come through My Spirit, says the Lord. Who and what can come against you, for you, I have called. For you, I have determined your destiny. For who can stop what I have ordained? says God. Fear not my daughter, because I am with you.

1994
Exodus 1

God is coming to deliver the Church from destruction. The church will grow and grow. There will be a time and SEASON where strong persecution shall come against the Church. There will be a holy remnant that will fear the Lord and will stand before God and help Him through prayer. God's army is growing stronger and mightier now. God will make provision for his people whom He has raised to fear Him.

There will be a birthing to those who I have impregnated with My power and vision to bring forth deliverance to My people. And You I have called to be a mid-wife, to help those who are carrying my seed (vision/purpose) to bring forth deliverance. Do not take what I am saying lightly. I will raise you up. You will not fear the enemy, because I am your protection. You will not fret, because the Lord Your God is with you and will bring forth victory.

October 1997
Philippians

Die Daughter, to your desires. Daughter, I desire to move you into that next place in Me. I will move you, daughter. Die to your thoughts. Have the mind of Christ; be content with where you are. I trust you. Now walk in a place of contentment and be settled in Me.

There are areas that will help me settle in you Lord.

Peace where I am; be encouraged where I am; walk in love where I am; have compassion where I am, show mercy where I am, and walk in oneness where I am. And the Great I AM will take you where you are supposed to be in Him.

The more I know Your Word, the more I am secure in Your will, because Your Word settles and stabilizes me in You.

I am a part of You, and when I am with You, I get to know what pleases You. I cannot, Lord, afford not to be with you each day. I must purpose in my heart to do Your will, and when I am not there, I pray to the Father I do not miss You. Lord, not my will but your will, Father, for my life.

September 1997
Season of Trials

He will lead us in a way we never been before. The Lord wants to take us where He wants us in this SEASON or TIME. He allows us to go into an unknown place to bring us to a place in Him that will change our lives. Things will begin to make sense to us soon. Our trust is in

Him only, and not in anyone else. We will trust in Him. A SEASON of trials has come to open our eyes to see the greatest of the Lord. God wants us to walk by faith. God wants to open up our heart, eyes and ears, so we can see and hear what the Spirit of the Lord is saying in this hour.

A time of warning and caution, Daughter of Zion. I have come to take you and My son to another place in Me. Why have you lost heart in what I have told you both? I have plans for you and My son. I will open your eyes and ears so you can hear Me. I love you, and I have promises for you, says God, and I will not forsake you. Daughter, it is done. Your financial situation is taken care of and nothing can stop that. I have blessed you and Duncan with My sovereign hands. Now listen, I will speak to you My instructions. Daughter, I have a move for you and your family. I need you to fast and pray. I will move you, but I want you to prepare your heart for such a move. Prepare in your heart and do not try to make this move happen. Be still and wait on Me. Keep that in your heart; you will be moving. I will speak to you both soon. Prepare the hearts of the children. Yes Daughter, you will see my hands.

Do not lose heart because you do not see My move. This move will be a sudden move. I will move you quickly in its SEASON. Daughter, I have settled your heart, and this will move you. You will be patient and WAIT. I have settled you heart. Now arise and shine; I have anointed you and my Son to set the captive free. You, Daughter, will walk in my healing power. A gift I gave you both, not one. You will see the sick and the broken hearted healed in My name. I will do this through you both. I have opened your eyes, and I have anointed you to open others to see Me. It is I, Daughter, who will work this good work in you both. Yes, you are My servants and messengers, who I am sending out. Daughter, you are settled in Me. I have settled you and My son to trust Me in this hour. It is not you; it is Me in You.

Now, love and trust Me daily for this vision to come to pass.

October 1997
Colossians 1:21-23

Daughter, you will set yourself apart for three days and on the third day you will come up where I am, and I will speak to you and show myself to you. I need you to come to this place. Why? Because I, Daughter, love you, and I want you to seek My face. I will do in you that I promised. Have I forgotten you, Daughter? No, I am with you; I am here to bring you to the place into which I called you and your family. Daughter, I love you and your family. I have a promise for you and My son. Do not give up on the vision and purpose I gave you. I have not forgotten you.

I love you Lord, You know I do not deserve that which you have given me. I need you. I am there for You. You know what I expect of you.

November 20, 1997

Father, thank You! Oh, how I love You, Jesus! Thank You. I love You, Holy Spirit, Thank you. I love You, Lord, and I love You. What more can I say? Your love, mercy, and guidance have kept me encouraged. I love Your Word. Let it dwell in My heart. I love You, Lord. Thank You. I am grateful this morning!

I will keep you Daughter, and I will use you for my glory. I will come to you in the midnight hour. I will do what I said I would do in your lives. I will bring forth My glory into this place, and you will see my hand in your lives. I love you, and I, says God, will move quickly. I will bring forth a change in this SEASON. I have already put things in motion. I say wait on the Lord, WAIT.

1997

Daughter, this situation you are in, I have put you there. Why? Because of My purpose, Daughter. Yes, you have been praying for years, but I have answered your prayers. I am giving you this child (a ministry to carry). I have impregnated you with My vision.

I must seek You with all my heart.

Press in. Do not move! You must go to the temple of the Lord. Come every day and seek Me.

January 1998
Ezekiel

God comes in His glory to speak to us, to give us instruction. He will stand us on our feet and set the path He has for us, and fill us with His Spirit.

Instruction to you, Daughter: You and My son will be sent to a rebellious house, and you will speak the truth to them. You will warn them of My judgment to come. I will place every word in your mouth. I will do this, Daughter, and they will reject and will not like you. I will mold you both into My image, and you will walk in strength and be of good courage. I will set order to your feet, and you shall shout My Words to the hilltop. I will feed you My Word only and prepare you to walk in greatness like never before. You will see My hand, Daughter, because you are the apple of My eye. I love You. Please listen when I move You. You will move with Me, and I will give you detailed instructions.

I must pray a prayer of intensity. A strong desire to seek the Lord with my whole heart. Deepen that desire, Father, in my heart, that I might seek Your face with my whole heart. I love you. I desire, Holy Spirit, to be aware of my seeking throughout the entire day. I desire to seek Him. I pray in Your Holy Name, Lord Jesus. I love you.

1998

Love is the key. I can walk in all the gifts and still be in bondage to my flesh, because I never locked into the love of Jesus. Without love, I have NOTHING.

I will work My love in you, Daughter. That is why it takes time and patience.

You must trust me during those hard times of your life; I am working in and through you. You must be able to take the love I am working in you to My people. I called you to love My people and to die daily in your flesh. I know you want my love.

Lord, I need your love; not my kind of love, but Your love. I love you; teach me Your ways, oh Lord, I pray.

I love you, Daughter; spend more time with Me.

1998

I will bring abundance, says God, and those who do not know Me will give forth their wealth, says God. This I shall do, says God. You question Me, Daughter, in what I have promised you. You will see the glory of the Lord. Daughter, a little while is only a little while in Me. Wait on Me and be of good courage, because I will perform My work in you and My son. Why? It is your destiny, the plans I have for you. I will change your course, says God, and you will see My hands. Yes, I will speak to you both. Settle in Me during this time and SEASON.

I truly love you, Lord. I love you with all my heart, I love you.

You will be financially set, because I will be glorified, says God. People you do not know will come to you. I will give you and My son favor. I, says God, will bring the blessing of the Lord. Why? Because I know you and your heart. I will honor it, and I will call upon you to carry out My task and finish it. Daughter, you have completed the work here. I must move you on, because it is time to arise and shine. The glory of the Lord is upon you. Now, let us go forward in that I have promised you. I promised you that I would use you in a mighty way.

This is the new beginning of what I have said to you. You will hear my instruction clearly. It is time for what I have placed in your hearts. You will see My hands. Daughter, wait on Me. I am moving!

1999

I give my heart to you, Lord, and I rejoice in Your people, who are willing to work and give to the kingdom. Let the people have a heart for You. We must bless and thank You for who you are in our lives, Lord.

Daughter of Zion, I have called you this day to exalt you before the sight of My people, says God. I will exalt you and Duncan before the people because the work I have for you is a great one. I will place you before the people, and the people will rejoice, for My hands are on you, says God. Watch My hands, Daughter; it is I who will bring it to pass. I have chosen you this day. I do, Daughter. Yes, Daughter I will complete this work.

First, know it is a time of completion in My promise to you. I have promised to anoint and use you for My glory. Suddenly, you will see the change. In addition, I will fill you to the brim with My Spirit. Yes, Daughter, the next 21 days is a separation and purification time for you. I will wash and speak to you during this time. I am doing this work in you. You and I will spend time in the Word, a holy, holy time. Take off your shoes, because you are on holy ground. Daughter, do not worry. I will keep you.

You must separate yourself, Daughter.

Daughter, I am still speaking to you. I have given you the authority and power to set the captives free. You will listen and obey. In order for Me to work through you, I will lead and guide you by My Holy Spirit. The Church, My people, will bring good tidings, and I have chosen a people who will surely be committed and faithful to bring forth My plans that I have for My Church. Daughter, I have given the plans to you and Duncan. I will show you My way. You must listen. Yes, Daughter, I looked for one who would stand in the gap, comfort, and guide My people. You have My love and compassion, you love to pray, and I hear your voice. Through listening to My voice and spending time with Me, you will hear me.

I love you, Lord.

2000
Hebrews

We must learn to endure, because there is a great reward in our endurance. We must endure in order to receive the promises, the blessing from the beginning to the end.

All my promises will come from your faith to believe in Me, and endure during this SEASON, to remain and do not become complacent where you are. Listen, Daughter, I will move you to the next place I have called you and Duncan. I will use Duncan to bring this to pass by touching his heart with My purposes for your lives. Now I want you to pray and endure in this SEASON. Trust Me, and I will bring all these things to pass.

Okay, Lord, I love You.

Oct 2000

Everything I have asked you to do will not be recognized by your hands, but by Mine, says the Lord. You will have My grace on your life in this SEASON. You will speak with authority, and you will see Me the midst. Lift up My Name.

There is a work that will not come out of my strength, but out of His. The Holy Spirit will totally guide us as a family. This is all God, no man. No one will cause this work. It will bring glory to Him only and grace to us to accomplish a task.

Yes, Daughter, you have been chosen by Me, says God, to accomplish this task and I rejoice in you, Daughter, because you shall surely complete it by My Grace, not by yourself. I have anointed you, Daughter, to set the captive free. Did I not tell you that I have anointed you for My people, and I have, Daughter? You will trust in Me totally, and no one else. I am who I said I am, rejoice in this day, for I have chosen you.

December 2000
Isaiah 2

A special task I have for you. A SEASON of carry a burden and pray for healing for my people. I will bring forth judgment. A watchman on the wall, you will pray, Daughter; night and day and day and night. I will cause you to come to this place. I need you to stay focused. I will hasten you to do this. Yes, Daughter, the move in this ministry is of Me. I will cause you and My son to rise to greatness in Me. I love you. You will not let man move you. It will only be Me, and I have already spoken to you both about My move. Yes, you are on the right track. You will focus on the task I have given you. Stay focused on My love.

I love You Lord, I love You.

2001
Habakkuk

Daughter, embrace God. I have given you and my son this vision for years. I have told you I will bring My judgment to this nation. Yes the Church. Daughter, I have not changed. Make it plain for My people. This shall come to pass in its TIME.

In other words, Lord You shall bring it to pass.

Yes, Daughter, I will. Do I delight in it? Says God. No. This is a burden in My heart. I want My people to turn from their wicked ways and pray, so I can heal this nation from their iniquities.

November 2001

I need You. I love You, Lord.

I am with you, Daughter. You are in the timing of the Lord. Stop looking at man and listen to Me. I will place in Duncan's heart where I want him. In the place where I am sending you, I will change your views on things in My body. The shepherd there is My son; He loves me. I will honor him with greatness, and I will move him on to other things I have planned for him. I will set you and Duncan there for a SEASON. I am moving very strongly in this hour. You will not worry about your children; you will see my hands upon all their lives soon. Yes, I will move quickly through the both of you and have already done a work in you as leaders. You, as leaders, now receive what I have for you. I am with you both. Now, fast and pray. I am speaking. Seven days you must fast.

2002
The Wells of Prayer- Isaiah 53

Daughter, you will heal the sick. You are called to teach others how to walk as I walk according to My Word. I came to earth to fulfill what My Father has spoken. Fulfillment is an action. Daughter, I have called you to fulfill My Word. Pray and speak My Word, and you will see the sick healed. Daughter, speak My Word and I will heal the sick.

Lord, you know I do not know how to take this, but by faith, I will be obedient. I do believe in Your word and I desire to please you. Teach me Your Way.

I will perform My word through you, as I have told you.

I love You, Lord.

2002

Daughter, My people are sinning against Me. I have come to get their attention. I have set you and My son in a place to be watchmen in the Church. You will speak My truth and deal with their wounds according to My Words. I will start My ministry and establish My Church through you both.

INSTRUCTIONS FOR YOUR WINDOWS

Working on your personal planner for peace of mind

- Please write the things you do throughout the day.

- This does not have to be a rigid schedule; you need some kind of guide to go by for each day.

- Note your day, the week and month will change with your season.

- If you do not have enough time in the day, then you need to look at your priorities.

- Please look at the practical ways of establishing your windows.

- Now you must purpose in your heart to clean your windows and get rid of the clutter in your temple.

- Remember this is only a guide to look at, so that you will know where you are each day! Some of us say we don't need to plan, or don't know how to, but if we make the effort to practice it for a season, we will find out we cannot live without it!!!

Practical Ways to Schedule your Windows

➢ **Seek the Lord first** so He can help you throughout the day. Remember He is the Lord of your Window. Every day and moment, He wants to be right there with you. You must **schedule yourself to get up a little earlier than usual.** This is your time to develop intimacy with God. Intimacy with God is not developed during your regular prayer time. It is not a onetime experience; you must get up early. If you get up at 6:00 a.m. for work, and you are off running, you need to get up at 5:00 a.m. You must learn how to abide/stay, and be still in His presence. You cannot rush in and out of God's presence. Learn how to wait on Him. Getting up at 5:00 a.m. gives you plenty of time to work through your sleepiness, thoughts for that day, and responsibilities. GET UP. If you get up and fall asleep, that is okay. We are working on discipline. Getting out of the bed first is the beginning of discipline, and then we will work on short prayers. The Holy Spirit can work you through the baby steps and help you grow. GET UP!

➢ **Make sure you take care of yourself.** If you do not have time for yourself in the morning, you are shortchanging yourself. You are valuable, and you need to treat yourself with value. This does not mean you get up taking two or three hours on yourself, but spending time getting yourself together. Some people get up and start moving the kids, cooking, and screaming in the morning. **They do not stop and spend some valuable quiet time for themselves, because they did not schedule themselves in their windows.** You can hear yourself saying, "Nobody thinks about me. I have to do everything. Who takes care of me? I'm tired of giving, and nobody gives back to me."

Can you hear yourself somewhere there? Why? Because you have not taken out the time to be, quiet and love yourself that morning.

➢ **Now we are ready to love and serve the spouse and kids.** Your spouse and children should have a window set just aside for them each day. Don't let your children run into your husband's window. They will learn to discipline their life after your pattern. Teach them to respect your daily schedule. Children only learn what you teach them. This is a good time to teach them Godly principles that can become a lifestyle for them, so they will not have to struggle in their windows when they get older.

➢ **Don't forget to pray with the spouse and children before they leave.** This is another very important window to schedule in your planner. They need the covering of the Lord for that day.

➢ **You must be accountable to someone who is mature and will help you with prayer, practical wisdom, and love.** For those who are not disciplined in writing in a planner and reading it every day, you need to work with a group or a friend that has this gift of organization. Partner up with someone to help you work on your planner and pray with you every day about your struggles. Call your partner and talk about the hardest part of your day, and where you need to make some changes in your life so you can feel comfortable with your schedule.

➤ **Make sure you have your spouse, children, job and ministry's calendars** so you can plan for the month. If any of the above does not have a planned calendar, you need to help them establish one, because if they do not have one, they will interrupt your windows and place unnecessary demands on you. **Someone else's lack of planning is not an emergency for you.** This is a very good principle to keep in your daily planning. Be gentle and loving when explaining to your family and others that they need to start organizing their lives so God can use them effectively.

➤ **In working with your windows, you must understand that our windows have daily, weekly, monthly, and yearly seasons.** There were times in my life when I was so busy that I could not keep up with my own windows. Let's use, as an example, one of the busiest months of the year. It is Christmas time, and I am running around for my family, the ministry, and trying to keep up with daily responsibilities. I find myself all over the place. **We must plan ahead the best we know how, so that we can enjoy this season, rather than having it become a time that we are so glad when it is over.** Another time is the summer, when the children are at home. **This threw me and everybody else out those windows.** I did not plan well for vacations and what the children would do for the summer. **It was a real mess.** This season was also very busy for me because we were leaders for a large camp for children every summer. It took planning, knowing how to delegate, and prayer to bring me through the summer season. Learn to prepare for your seasons before they come

Appendix
Sample Windows Sheet

1.	4:00 AM
2.	4:30 AM
3.	5:00 AM
4.	5:30 AM
5.	6:00 AM
6.	6:30 AM
7.	7:00 AM
8.	7:30 AM
9.	8:00 AM
10.	8:30 AM
11.	9:00 AM
12.	9:30 AM
13.	10:00 AM
14.	10:30 AM
15.	11:00 AM
16.	11:30 AM
17.	12:00 PM
18.	12:30 PM
19.	1:00 PM
20.	1:30 PM

21.	2:00 PM
22.	2:30 PM
23.	3:00 PM
24.	3:30 PM
25.	4:00 PM
26.	4:30 PM
27.	5:00 PM
28.	5:30 PM
29.	6:00 PM
30.	6:30 PM
31.	7:00 PM
32.	7:30 PM
33.	8:00 PM
34.	8:30 PM
35.	9:00 PM
36.	9:30 PM
37.	10:00 PM
38.	10:30 PM
39.	11:00 PM
40.	11:30 PM
41.	12:00:00 AM (midnight)

Rules for Tonight

Set a time of rest for you TONIGHT

You are not allowed in the kitchen.

You MUST REST and have FUN!!

You will not talk about work or ministry.

You are not allowed to do anything.

You must REST and RELAX!

You will not worry about your children.

You WILL eat as much as you want!

NO PHONE CALLS!

NO BEEPERS / NO CELL PHONES!

This is your time of rest!

Manufactured by Amazon.com
Columbia, SC
10 April 2017